# The

# LEARNING

# *Solution*

# The

# LEARNING

# *Solution*

## What to Do If Your Child Has Trouble with Schoolwork

## Nathan Naparstek, Ph.D.

AVON BOOKS ◆ NEW YORK

THE LEARNING SOLUTION: WHAT TO DO IF YOUR CHILD HAS TROUBLE WITH SCHOOLWORK is an original publication of Avon Books. This work has never before appeared in book form.

AVON BOOKS
A division of
The Hearst Corporation
1350 Avenue of the Americas
New York, New York 10019

Library of Congress Cataloging in Publication Data:

Naparstek, Nathan.
  The learning solution: what to do if your child has trouble with schoolwork / Nathan Naparstek.
      p.   cm.
Includes bibliographical references.
1. Learning disabled children—Education—United States.
2. Education—Parent participation—United States.   3. Home and school—United States.   I. Title.
LC4705.N36   1995                                                              94-32742
371.91'0973—dc20                                                                  CIP

First Avon Books Trade Printing: March 1995

# Acknowledgments

I want to thank all the people who assisted me in writing this book. First, I want to thank my friend David Porush for reviewing my early drafts and providing insightful suggestions. I also appreciate the support and confidence he had in this book. Second, I want to thank my editor, Lisa Considine, for providing excellent advice and being a pleasure to work with. I could not imagine having a better editor. Third, I want to thank all the teachers, administrators, parents, students, and colleagues who have enriched my understanding of children's learning.

Special thanks go to my parents, who gave me the educational opportunities that they never had. I also want to thank my children, Eli, Rachel, and Joseph, for being understanding about the time I have spent on this book.

Most of all, I want to thank my wife, Denise, who at the end of the day would always find time to review my drafts and provide me with new ideas. Without her assistance, I could not have completed this book.

# CONTENTS

### ■ ■ ■

# INTRODUCTION

### ■ ■ ■

Have you or a friend of yours received a letter like this?

*Dear Mr. and Mrs. Johnson,*

*Your son David is having difficulty succeeding in the fourth grade this year. We would like to have him tested by the school psychologist to see if we need to repeat him in the fourth grade or if he can benefit from special educational services.*

*Sincerely yours,*
*Mrs. Jones*
*Fourth Grade Teacher*

Mr. and Mrs. Johnson reacted with shock and anger to this letter. Nobody had warned them that David was having such a hard time in school. Nobody had let the Johnsons know about the effectiveness of school interventions such as retention or special education. Furthermore, Mr. and Mrs. Johnson were not consulted about alternative interventions that are more effective.

The Johnsons were so unprepared for this letter that they had no idea how to begin dealing with David's teacher or the school psychologist. They had many doubts, but felt that they had to trust blindly that David's school would deal with his problems positively and make the best decisions for him. Sometimes schools are equipped to deal with children's learning problems, but sometimes they aren't.

If your child has a problem learning in school, whether or not the school has diagnosed it, this book is designed to deliver knowledge into your hands. It is a cliché to say that education is the key to your child's future, but like many clichés, it holds a powerful truth. Schools are well-meaning institutions, but they are still institutions. The love and concern you have for your child is an invaluable tool for helping him or her through a tough time. By adding knowledge to the equation, you will be well-equipped to become a powerful partner in aiding your child through a difficult period of growth. In the end, you should be the one to decide whether the schools are dealing effectively with your child's learning problems or not. You should be the one to decide just what you can do about it. Your knowledge will make you a most effective partner with the schools in helping your child.

This book is written for parents like Mr. and Mrs. Johnson who have children like David who are not succeeding in school. Many parents of children with learning difficulties are angry because they lack information and guidance on how to help their children succeed in school. Perhaps you have already been down the road with the schools for a couple of years and are beginning to feel frustration at the lack of visible improvement in your child. You may feel that the school system is not responsive, but perhaps that's because you lack the knowledge to ask the questions that could lead to a better, more effective treatment. This book provides you with the questions that you need to ask yourself, your child, and your child's teachers, in addition to specific strategies that you can use to improve your child's learning.

Some parents believe that schools have all the tools that are needed to "fix" their children's learning difficulties. However, parents simply cannot passively sit back and expect a school system by itself to "correct" their child's learning problems. Getting a child help through the school system is not the same thing as getting your car serviced at a repair shop. Most educators buy into this kind of "service mentality" that assumes that all a child needs to improve is to get a service. Very few people question whether the service will be beneficial or harmful for the child.

Most of the available research indicates that intervention programs offered by public school systems often fail to improve children's learning significantly. These programs include remedial reading, remedial math, and special educational services. They are usually insufficient because they do not provide sufficient individual assistance. Intensive one-on-one programs are the most effective way of improving the academic performance of children with learning difficulties. Children with learning problems benefit significantly from individualized tutoring services provided by well-trained educational professionals.

Having a professional tutor provide intensive individual assistance for a child is an ideal situation. However, public schools do not typically provide this type of assistance for the simple reason that they cannot afford to hire the staff needed to work individually with children. Similarly, most parents also lack the financial resources to pay for a private tutor. Hence, most children lack access to the most effective means of help for their learning difficulties.

A major goal of this book is to suggest viable alternative educational strategies for children who do not have access to a professional private tutor. The good news is that parents who receive the proper instruction can themselves serve as effective tutors and educational supports for their children. Many parents do make an effort to tutor their children, but abandon the attempt because of stressful and unproductive experiences. Parents can successfully instruct their children if they educate themselves about strategies for promoting positive and effective tutoring situations. Most parents are also unaware of the fact that they are their children's first teachers. Parents teach children safety rules, behavior rules, language skills, social skills, and survival skills.

Other goals of this book are to increase your knowledge about the resources offered by schools and to maximize the effectiveness of your interactions with school personnel. All parents, teachers, and school administrators want to see children succeed in school. Almost all educational decisions made by schools are made with good intentions. Some of these decisions will be helpful for children and others will not. This book will attempt to guide you in judging which programs or educational decisions will be beneficial for your child.

I hope that this book will provide you with the motivation, skills, and confidence to become more effectively involved in your child's education.

# 1.

# COMMON LEARNING DIFFICULTIES

## What They Are and How They Affect School Progress

■ ■ ■

*When Mrs. Davis, heard from the school that her son Johnny was "Learning Disabled," she asked Johnny's teacher what a Learning Disability was. The teacher told her it meant that Johnny has a learning problem. Mrs. Davis then asked the teacher what the learning problem was. The teacher told her that Johnny was not completing his work. Mrs. Davis asked why Johnny was not doing his work. The teacher was frustrated by this conversation and replied, "I just told you, it's because he has a Learning Disability."*

## DEFINITION OF A LEARNING PROBLEM

What is a learning problem? A learning problem exists when there is a difference between peoples' expectations and the child's academic performance. A child can only be identified as having a learning problem when he or she has failed to meet someone's expectation for academic success. The expectations that need to be explored are those of teacher, parent, and child. A conflict in expectations among any of these individuals will lead to stress and possible conflict in a child's educational environment.

Expectations for performance occur in any work situation. At work, your boss expects certain things of you, and you expect certain things of yourself. When you don't perform up to the expectations of your boss, you are either reprimanded, demoted, or fired. The difference between the workplace and the school is that your child can't be fired; by law, he or she must be educated until age 16. However, a child can be demoted, or transferred to an alternate program.

In school, expectations exist in the academic, social, and behavioral realms. In exploring expectations for each category, it is important to determine where they come from and whether they are appropriate for your child. Expectations can also be divided in terms of "core expectations" that have to be fulfilled, and "optional expectations" that are not as critical.

Teachers and parents need to have appropriate expectations for a child's performance in each area. No one should look at the child as the only source of a learning difficulty. Sometimes a child's learning difficulties are the result of being presented with tasks that are too advanced, a curriculum that is disorganized, or poor teaching. You want to make sure that any learning difficulties are not the result of inappropriate expectations for your child's performance. If your boss asks you to complete a monstrous task in a very short time, is your failure the result of your incompetence or unreasonable expectations? It would be equally unreasonable to automatically classify a new student from a foreign country as having a learning problem. This student needs time to adjust to a new language and culture before becoming successful. Typically such a student's difficulties would be due to language and cultural issues, not learning ones.

Different school districts may also have different expectations for skill acquisition. For example, schools in wealthy communities tend to have a more advanced curriculum and higher expectations than schools in less affluent areas. The child who is experiencing "learning difficulties" at a well-funded school could be an average student at a less affluent one. Having a learning difficulty can therefore be a relative term. We cannot view a child's learning difficulties in isolation from the child's environment and the expectations in that environment.

## Teacher Expectations

Classroom teachers have several core expectations of students in the classroom. These include the ability to attend to instructions, complete independent work assignments, complete homework assignments, pass classroom and standard-ized academic tests, and follow classroom rules for appropriate behavior. Core expectations are the basic mini-mum performance the child needs to demonstrate to be a successful member of a classroom. Failure to meet any of the core expectations is likely to lead to some form of negative feedback from the classroom teacher to the child and the parents.

Optional expectations refer to situations beyond those of minimum competency. Ideally, teachers would like to see a child do more than the absolute minimum required to pass. For example, it would be nice if a child was reading above grade level and always handed in neat assignments. Although most teachers would like all students to excel in their class-room performance, students in any one class will be likely to exhibit a wide range of accomplishment. Therefore, teachers have core minimum expectations, and optional expectations that reflect the need to deal with this range of skill levels.

A teacher's expectations for specific learning accomplish-ments in the classroom are often determined by the educa-tional curriculum set by the state education department and the school district. Many school districts have curriculum de-partments that provide information concerning expectations for learning at different grade levels. Children are supposed to master the information in textbooks that reflect this curric-ulum. Teachers also determine their expectations for a partic-ular child by relating that child's current performance to the average skill level in the classroom.

## *Parent Expectations*

Parents and teachers may have similar core expectations. However, if there is a difference, it could understandably lead to parent-teacher conflict. A child's mother and father may themselves disagree on expectations for performance in the classroom. Parental disagreements can obviously complicate efforts to coordinate a successful academic program.

Clearly, parents and teachers have different perspectives when considering the problems of a particular child. Teachers view a child as a member of a group, while the parents are more likely to view the child as an individual. Teacher expec-tations tend to be more influenced by group variables, and parent expectations by individualistic ones. Teachers are able to directly compare a child's performance to that of classmates because they understand what typical performance is for a child at a specific grade level. Parents lack this knowledge simply because they are not in the classroom, and probably aren't intimate with how other children in the class are doing. Parents tend to develop their standards of performance from their individual experiences or culture. For example, parents who grew up getting C's in school may feel it's okay for their child to have a C average. For other parents, nothing less than an A average is acceptable.

Parental expectations are a key and often overlooked variable in looking at learning issues. In my 13 years as a school psychologist, I have found that most children tend to live up to parental expectations for academic success. However, it is important that these expectations be consistent with the child's abilities. Consider your own work situation; imagine what it feels like when your boss has confidence in your abilities. Now contrast this situation to what it feels like to work for a boss who routinely assumes you're not up to the job. Which boss would you like to work for?

Our expectations have to be adjusted to the unique qualities of each child. Each child has individual strengths and weaknesses. Just because an older sibling was able to read at the age of five does not mean that a younger sibling will also be able to do so. The classroom teacher can be a good source for determining if parental expectations are consistent with a child's abilities. Based on experience with many children at a given age, the classroom teacher has a good idea of what skills are developmentally appropriate.

## *The Child's Expectations*

Your child's expectations develop as a result of individual personality characteristics, home environment, and school experiences. Most children compare themselves to their classmates and expect to at least keep up with them. Even kindergarten and first grade students are aware of how they compare to their classmates. Parental and teacher expectations tend to be incorporated into the child's belief system. However, when parent expectations and teacher expectations differ, the child will experience some educational stress. The stress will be even greater when the child's expectations differ from those of the adults. In this situation, your child has to either change his or her expectations, or choose to disregard those of the adults. If your child chooses the latter approach, significant behavioral difficulties could ensue. It is important that the adults' expectations be realistic. Many children with learning difficulties also have emotional and behavioral problems because they have been exposed to expectations that they do not believe they can meet.

On the other hand, sometimes problems result from adult expectations that the child perceives as too low. Teachers and parents can underestimate a child's abilities and present an academic program that is not challenging or that is simply boring for a child. This is often the case with gifted children who are faced with an academic curriculum that is not sufficiently novel to hold their interest.

Some children may have high levels of aspiration and may have the goal of being significantly above average in their academic performance. Such a child who fails to meet these expectations will experience stress. In this situation, the child's "learning problem" will be alleviated by providing more appropriate expectations. In many situations, the teacher, the child, and the parents will need to meet and set up clear, consistent, and realistic expectations for classroom performance.

## BEWARE OF LABELS

*Mrs. Bell tells her neighbor that her daughter, Mary, has been diagnosed as having "Dyslexia." The neighbor asks what "Dyslexia" means. Mrs. Bell reports that it means Mary has a reading problem. The neighbor then asks, "Why didn't her school just say that Mary had a reading problem?" Mrs. Bell says, "I think they just like to use them fancy words to make themselves look important."*

How are learning problems described? Schools often use labels such as "Learning Disabled," "Speech and Language Impaired," "Emotionally Disturbed," or "Mentally Retarded" to describe a child's learning difficulties. Schools employ these labels to classify children for various educational programs and for state record-keeping purposes. These labels are hypothetical terms used to describe a child's general difficulties. They tell you in vague, nonspecific ways that your child is deficient in some way. They never tell you how your child excels. Educational labels are not like medical labels that have a specific origin and course of treatment.

Educational labels often become a trap when they are used to explain or define a child's actions. This is circular reasoning that doesn't really explain anything. To say that your child has learning problems because she has a "Learning Disability" does not tell you anything new. However, it provides you with a pseudo-medical condition to explain why your child has difficulty learning. Sometimes parents like to have their child labeled with a handicapping condition because it identifies a possible explanation for the learning problems. In some cases a label such as "Learning Disabled" or "Dyslexic" makes the parents feel better, since they now "know" what the problem is. These parents trust that the "experts" will be able to come up with ways to solve their child's learning problems. Unfortunately, those of you who have already been down this road know that there are few quick fixes and the labeling has no positive impact on your child's education.

The use of a label may distract a parent from looking at meaningful causes for a child's learning difficulties. Perhaps your child does not have a learning problem, but the curriculum in the classroom is inappropriately difficult and the child is unable to integrate it with prior experiences. The use of a label may have harmful consequences because of its effect on parental and teacher expectations. People may have lower expectations for a child labeled "Learning Disabled." People may expect a child who is labeled as "Emotionally Handicapped" to present behavioral difficulties. A child who becomes aware of the handicapping label may feel unable to succeed in school because of this pseudo-medical condition that interferes with learning. Having a handicapping label does not tell a teacher or a parent how to plan an educational program. Planning an educational program can only be done by looking at the individual needs of the child.

Getting a child labeled is perhaps the most uncomfortable experience a parent can experience with a school system, so it helps to be informed about the process. School districts attempt to convince parents to accept this label by saying that it can be withdrawn if the child makes progress in future years. There are two problems with this logic:

**1.** Even if the label is officially withdrawn, the child could still be tainted by it. Imagine this situation in a work environment: Mr. Bryant's boss writes in his file that he is a poor worker and then later says that he is now a good worker. Most people who later consult his file will think that he is a poor worker or that he is predisposed to being one. The same thing can happen to a child's academic file.

**2.** The label is usually not withdrawn, and the child carries it throughout their school career.

## THE ORIGIN OF LEARNING DIFFICULTIES

*Mr. Ames was told that his daughter was "Learning Disabled." His next thought was "How could this happen? What did I do wrong?" Mr. Ames wanted to blame himself for his daughter's learning problems. He felt that he could have done something to prevent them. He did not understand that most learning problems have a complex origin that are beyond the control of most parents.*

What are the origins of learning problems? Often it is hard to determine how or why a child has developed a learning difficulty. It is important that you as a parent view these difficulties as having complex origins. People are not machines on which you can run a diagnostic check that will explain exactly how the problem was caused and what you need to do to repair it. You could not ask a school psychologist to find out what is wrong with your child and to fix it. The best that a school psychologist can do is to come up with a possible explanation for the difficulty and suggest possible interventions. Knowing the probable origin of your child's learning problem is only useful when it leads to ways of improving the learning situation.

You need to develop a healthy attitude about the origin of your child's learning difficulties. Don't deny your child's feelings. Let the child know that you accept the fact that he or she is having difficulty completing schoolwork. Let your child know that you understand how he or she feels. Don't forget that it is *your child* who has to struggle every day in school. It is easy to take your child's lack of success in school too personally and even to become depressed over it. It is important to be aware of your own feelings about your child's difficulties so you can acknowledge your child's feelings and provide emotional support.

Some parents view the child's lack of academic success as a reflection of their lack of success as parents. These parents blame themselves for the child's difficulties and feel remorse about the things they did or didn't do. A learning difficulty is *not* the result of forgetting to take your child to the library last Saturday or failing to spend enough time working with your child. Instead, it is the result of many complex environmental and genetic interactions.

A related issue is that of "who" has the problem. For example, the "hyperactive child" may not have a "problem"; instead, the people who must interact with the child may have the "problem." Many hyperactive children are efficient learners but disturb their peers and teachers by their high level of activity. In many situations, teacher, peers, and parents must work to increase their understanding and tolerance for the child's high activity level.

Children's learning difficulties can be viewed as being primarily due to factors within the child, the home environment, or the school environment. But before examining any of these areas as the source of the learning difficulties, it is important to first rule out the possibility of physiological factors affecting your child's academic performance.

## Physiological Factors

If you suspect your child has a learning problem, you should take the child to a pediatrician for a complete physical examination. On occasion, a child may have a medical condition, such as a seizure disorder, allergies, or chemical imbalance, that has been previously undetected. A physician may be able to detect a physiological problem and recommend some medical assistance. When I make a psychological assessment of a child, I am very conservative and will recommend the child for a neurological or complete medical evaluation if I have even the slightest concern over these issues. I want to rule out any health issue that can affect a child's learning. The neurologist is only useful in evaluating a child's gross neurological functioning and determining if a seizure disorder is present. If the neurological impairment is minor, the neurologist probably will fail to provide a firm diagnosis. Keep in mind that neurologists and other physicians are not educators. Therefore, you cannot expect educational recommendations from them.

Genetic factors could be involved in a child's learning difficulties. Down's syndrome is a well-known condition that is the result of the child having an extra chromosome and is associated with physical and cognitive limitations. Other genetic syndromes, such as Turner's or Klinefelter's, also limit a child's capacity to learn. A lot of research suggests that general intellectual abilities are inherited—for example, identical twins raised apart appear to have a closer level of intellectual functioning than fraternal twins raised in the same family. The research on specific learning problems is less conclusive, but there appears to be a genetic link. In my clinical practice, I have often seen children with reading or math difficulties whose parents have experienced a similar difficulty.

Learning difficulties can also be the result of trauma during birth, childhood illnesses, or personal injury. If a child is without oxygen for any significant time, it can result in the permanent destruction of brain cells. Sometimes the lack of oxygen could be the result of complications during birth or an operation in which general anesthesia is applied. Brain cells don't regenerate when they are destroyed. Each child is born with a limited number of brain cells, and unlike skin and other tissues, they do not grow back when damaged.

A significant head injury can also result in the destruction of brain cells. Many children suffer head injuries because they don't wear helmets when riding bicycles. A helmet cushions a child's brain from the impact of a head injury during a bicycle accident.

## *Environmental Factors*

Environmental experiences have a strong effect on a child's learning. Many learning difficulties could be the result of complications involved with the mother's pregnancy. It is important for a pregnant woman to obtain the proper nutrition and avoid the intake of harmful substances such as nicotine, alcohol, and other drugs that can harm the fetus or increase the risk of a premature birth.

After birth, it is important for a child to be exposed to a stable home environment that provides for physical, nutritional, emotional, and learning needs. Home should be an environment that models and encourages processes related to learning. Parents can create such an environment by reading stories out loud to the child, having books in the house, asking the child questions about learning activities, providing the child with opportunities to see educationally relevant materials in places such as a museum, and, most important, conveying to the child the importance of education and learning.

## School Factors

Learning problems can be the result of presenting a child with material that is too advanced. For this child, it may be beneficial to wait awhile before trying to teach certain concepts. Not every child in a classroom is at the same readiness level for learning various skills. Presenting a young child with "impossible" tasks leads a child to doubt their ability to learn in school. Besides hurting your child's self-esteem, it may also cause your child to develop a negative attitude about school. It is not easy to have a good attitude about a situation in which you experience a lot of failure.

Consultation with teachers, administrators, the school psychologist, and educational experts such as college professors, may be needed to evaluate the effect of a possible inappropriate school environment on the child's learning difficulties. These individuals are the sources for information regarding the appropriate expectations for someone in your child's learning environment. As a concerned parent, you have to investigate the characteristics of your child's learning environment to make sure that it is appropriate.

# DIAGNOSING LEARNING PROBLEMS

Psychologists, such as James Rest, sometimes use models to explain why people behave the way they do. These same models can be applied to learning situations to explain why a child has difficulty learning. Below are four learning components that I derived from Rest's model to explain why a child fails to succeed in school:

## *Attending Component*

Some children have difficulty listening to directions and paying attention to the essential details of work assignments. Problems in this area can be due to difficulties sustaining concentration, distractibility, or vision and hearing problems. A child cannot be successful in an academic assignment without understanding the directions for completing it.

You cannot necessarily teach a child to pay better attention, but you can teach a child to recognize the central aspects of a learning situation that need to be attended to, or motivate the child to maximize their ability to pay attention. You can also alter the learning environment to help the child compensate for learning difficulties. This can be done either by exposing the child to less information or by breaking the information down into smaller parts that are easier to attend to.

## *Ability Component*

Does your child have the ability to successfully complete the task if he or she correctly understands the directions? If the answer is no, we have to look at the skills your child is missing. It is also essential to understand your child's abilities in an academic area. A child's ability to succeed on academic tasks depends on prior experience with similar tasks and on intelligence.

Familiarity with specific content or skill areas can be accomplished through long-range planning. If you know that your child will need certain skills for next year's tasks, it may be a good idea to work on them during the current year or in the summer. For example, if multiplication will be taught during the next school year, it may be a good idea for you and your child to practice simple multiplication tasks during the summer. Timely tutoring, remedial instruction, and good teaching can help to prepare a child for future learning.

Very often, a child needs a certain level of intellectual ability to successfully complete an academic assignment. A child with below-average intellectual ability will have difficulty recognizing the correct strategies for solving problems. Such a child will also have difficulty generalizing the use of strategies to new situations. For example, Jane could learn how to use the best strategy to add "11 + 9", but would become confused when adding "22 + 9". She was able to apply the concept of "carrying" in the former situation but could not generalize it to the latter one.

Intellectual ability is not something that can be specifically taught. Instead, it is a broad ability based on a child's genetic inheritance and long-term environmental experiences. At this time, no effective programs have been developed to accelerate the intellectual functioning of school-aged children. When intellectual acceleration is observed, it is usually the result of significant environmental changes. Most of the significant gains in intellectual development appear to be the result of intervention programs that are started during the preschool years. Therefore, if you are dealing with a school-aged child with intellectual impairment, the educational issues will revolve around compensating for these difficulties instead of improving intellectual functioning. For example, a child with impaired intellectual functioning will experience difficulty applying skills in new situations. That child will need extra instruction to learn how to solve tasks in each new and specific situation. With creative compensation strategies like those discussed in Chapter Six, you can help most intellectually impaired children make significant improvement in their school performance. Being intellectually impaired does not mean that your child cannot be successful, it simply means that the child will need to work hard to compensate for their deficits. By definition, most children have average intelligence. However, if you are concerned about this issue, you could contact a school psychologist to obtain a psychological assessment.

## *Decision Component*

Does your child want to solve the task? Does your child have motivation to succeed in school? Some children can accurately interpret the details of an academic task and know how to complete it successfully, yet they do not want to solve it because of a lack of interest or motivation. This component is most common to the child who is experiencing emotional difficulties. Some children may refuse to complete school assignments because they are angry about something that happened at home. Other children may refuse to complete work assignments because they do not perceive them as important. Some children simply don't complete schoolwork because there is no significant consequence for not doing it.

Parents have an important role to play in the issues of motivation and task persistence. Some children will be unresponsive to teachers' efforts to motivate them. I often find that the child's parents are significantly better than the school at motivating maximum school performance because they have a stronger emotional connection. Your approval and encouragement can mean a lot to your children. Parents also have more resources than educators to respond to their child's school performance through the use of rewards and punishments.

## *Execution Component*

Perhaps your child already wants to solve the task. The concern is whether your child has the personality characteristics and emotional strength to follow through on their decision to work on the task. Your child needs to have the ability to deal effectively with frustration or anxiety that results from working on tasks. Your child also needs to concentrate on the task to complete it successfully. Children who are easily distracted may have problems with task completion. A hyperactive child, for example, may be able to follow directions, use the appropriate strategies, and have the desire to complete tasks, but is unsuccessful in school because of a breakdown in the final stage. The hyperactive child may simply not be able to sit in a chair long enough to complete the academic assignment.

Some children are unsuccessful in school because they

have difficulty dealing effectively with the anxiety that results from working on academic tasks. They typically withdraw from the task in order to avoid feeling anxious. The anxiety could be the result of emotional or self-esteem issues. In this situation, your child may benefit from counseling services.

Physical problems, such as a child's inability to write at a normal rate of speed, can also interfere with the ability to demonstrate knowledge in the classroom. It is important that your child has the physical capability to complete assignments. The inability to do so will be extremely stressful for your child. In this situation, you have to make sure that your child's teachers are aware of the physical impediment and that steps are taken to adjust to it, such as requiring fewer assignments to be completed or allowing the child to use aids, such as a computer, to complete them.

A failure in any of the proposed components will lead to learning problems for a child. The four components are closely related to one another. For example, a weak content knowledge, poor motivation, and a high anxiety level will all interfere with a child's ability to pay attention to directions. Similarly, a lack of skills and difficulty in following directions will affect a child's motivation to complete work.

## COMMON SCHOOL DIFFICULTIES

Most school difficulties are related to deficits in reading skills, symptoms associated with Attention Deficit Hyperactivity Disorder, or emotional problems. The nature and origin of these difficulties are explored on the following pages.

### *Reading*

Most children identified in schools as having a "learning disability" are labeled as such because of problems in reading. Typically, such a child has at least average vocabulary for his or her age, but is deficient in the ability to sound out words. Reading is the most important skill a child can acquire in school, and reading impairment is directly related to difficulties in the rest of a child's academic subject areas. Obviously, a child who cannot adequately read the instructions for completing a task will have difficulty with written assignments. A child's progress in social studies or science will be impeded if the child cannot successfully read the textbooks. Reading difficulties can also affect a child's progress in seemingly unrelated areas such as math. Though math is numerically based, the child needs to be able to read and understand written directions to complete math assignments. This is especially true when a child is working on math word problems.

Young children with reading problems usually have difficulty seeing the relationship between written text (i.e., the letters) and oral language (i.e., the letter sounds). They often have to memorize the whole word to sound it out because they can't put the letter sounds together to form a word. Children with reading difficulties read with hesitation and at a slow pace. Reading is a difficult activity for them, unlike the average adult who reads words quickly and automatically. Most adults process the words so rapidly that they spend almost no time attending to the individual letters. In contrast, the inefficient reader has to spend a lot of time attending to word parts because they are not automatically meaningful. Because reading is such a slow and laborious process, the poor reader may develop a negative attitude toward reading. Now the teacher has to deal not only with the reading difficulty but also with the negative attitudes it creates. Difficulties in reading may lead to difficulties in self-esteem and the child's self-perception as a learner.

It is important to have an accurate understanding of the origin of your child's reading problem. This understanding will guide you to appropriate places for assistance. A poor understanding of the problem can lead you to experiment with unproven strategies that have little research to support them. Some people, for example, believe that reading problems are due to vision or visual-perception deficits. They believe that children usually see letters or words backwards. If that were true, it would be hard to imagine how these same children could negotiate the world around them well enough to walk through an open door; wouldn't they possibly confuse the floor with the ceiling? While some reading difficulties could be vision-related, almost all the available research indicates that reading deficits are strongly related to language development.

Theoretically, anything that affects language development could place the child at risk for future reading difficulties. Problems using language could be the result of a child's ear infections, lack of exposure to good use of language by parents, or complications in how the brain organizes language. A young child who experiences many ear infections may have difficulty hearing and paying attention to the sounds of letters and distinguishing them from one another. If parents don't engage the child with stimulating conversation, the child may develop a weak vocabulary, fail to understand the meanings of many words, develop weak grammatical skills, and ultimately lack a good foundation for reading.

Some children still experience language difficulties in spite of normal hearing and stimulating conversation at home. These children appear to have a dysfunction in the brain resulting from a head injury or an inherited condition. You could think of the brain as an electrical system with wires for communicating and sending messages. A child may have irregularities in the brain "wiring" that cause messages to be distorted. Such children will need a lot of assistance compensating for faulty interpretations.

Language difficulties can be observed after the child is about two years of age. The infant's early years are viewed as a critical period for acquiring various skills. If you suspect a difficulty in your child's language development, it is important to take the child to a pediatrician to rule out the effect of ear infections. An ear infection causes the sounds the child hears to be similar to sounds heard under water. This can impede your child's development of language skills (specifically in the area of phonics or letter sounds), and interfere with the child's ability to pay attention to what is heard. Many children who experience early ear infections later develop a habit or ingrained pattern of not paying attention to what they hear. These attending difficulties can persist even after full hearing returns.

## Attention Deficit Hyperactivity Disorder

Another major area of difficulties for school-aged children relates to problems in sustaining their attention, impulsivity, and overactivity. DSM-IV (*The Diagnostic and Statistical Manual* of the American Psychiatric Association) has a name for these types of problems: Attention Deficit Hyperactivity Disorder (ADHD). Until recently, ADHD was simply a clinical label to describe children who exhibit certain types of behaviors. However, federal legislation has recently established it as a condition that can be used under the label of "other Health Impaired" to classify a child for special educational services, which are discussed in Chapter Two.

ADHD is usually detected before the age of seven, and occurs in only about 3 to 5 percent of the population. However, it constitutes more than half the referrals of children to mental health clinics. Boys constitute the vast majority of children diagnosed as having ADHD because their aggressive behaviors tend to be more noticeable than those of girls.

Psychologists and physicians used to think that as a child approached adolescence, he or she simply outgrew ADHD. It is now viewed as a chronic condition that most children do not outgrow. Generally, a child's activity level does decline, but the problems with sustaining attention and impulsivity remain. There is also a tendency for parents who themselves have ADHD to have children with ADHD. Most children (70 to 80 percent) with this label do not have learning difficulties in school. Instead, they have difficulties completing work assignments in a timely manner and following school rules for behavior. A child with ADHD is sometimes described as being like a well-built car with faulty brakes. The child is often capable of learning but has difficulty with putting the brakes on impulses. The child gets into trouble by frequently forgetting to think before acting. For example, the child will get out of the assigned seat to talk to another student instead of working on an assignment. The child is aware of the rules about sitting at the desk and working on the assignment, but is thinking about discussing some television show that was on last night with a friend. Instead of waiting to consider the effect of the behavior (i.e., the teacher will yell at the child, and the work won't get done), the child goes with the immediate impulse (i.e., talking with a friend).

According to Russell Barkley, one of the most respected psychologists on the subject of ADHD, the child with ADHD is easily bored. Barkley believes ADHD is a motivational disorder in that the child will not easily give attention to tasks that the child does not find interesting. Therefore, much to a parent's dismay, the child with ADHD will be attentive when playing Nintendo or watching a favorite television program, but will be inattentive in the classroom. Children with ADHD need constant positive reinforcement and novelty to keep them engaged in classroom-related activities.

While difficulties in paying attention and hyperactivity are often associated with each other, many children have difficulty paying attention but are not hyperactive. This disorder is called Attention Deficit Hyperactivity Disorder—primarily Inattentive type.

The diagnosis of ADHD is a subjective process. It is usually diagnosed through the use of behavioral checklists, rating scales, parental reports, teacher reports, and observations of the child in the classroom. It is especially difficult for physicians to diagnose because ADHD children tend to be on their best behavior in relatively novel (i.e., interesting) situations, such as a doctor's office.

There is some evidence that ADHD has a physiological basis. The best evidence for this physiological link comes from an experimental study in Denmark. The subjects with ADHD were injected with a radioactive substance and then given a computerized tomography (CAT scan), which takes an opaque picture of one's brain. The results indicated that all the people with ADHD showed a reduced blood flow at the frontal lobe of the brain. Further confirmation for the involvement of the frontal lobe comes from another study that used a positron emissions tomography (PET scan), currently the most advanced technology for examining the brain. The subjects in this study were also injected with a radioactive substance, and the tests again showed reduced activity in the frontal lobe. Simply put, the frontal lobe of people with ADHD appears to be less active than that of people without ADHD. The frontal lobe area of the brain is thought to deal with decision-making processes and is related to attending skills.

It is not practical, nor does it appear to be safe, to inject a radioactive substance into a child's brain to see if the frontal lobe has a lower than average activity level! Therefore, it is unlikely that ADHD will be able to be identified by physiological measures in the immediate future. This means that diagnosis of ADHD will continue to be a subjective process. It also means that ADHD can be construed as a pseudo-medical label like "learning disability" or "emotionally disturbed."

The treatment of ADHD typically involves behavior modification strategies that focus on promoting positive behaviors and discouraging undesirable ones. Diets to control for sugar intake, such as the Feingold diet, have little effect on the functioning of children with ADHD. It's possible that diets may be helpful for some children, but this group of children represents an extremely small percentage of the children labeled with ADHD.

Strange as it may seem, pediatricians or child psychiatrists also prescribe stimulant medication such as Ritalin, Dexedrine, or Cylert, to increase a child's "on task" behavior and reduce high activity levels. The current theory is that ADHD is a physiological problem. Researchers believe that the metabolism of ADHD children's brain cells is different from that of the typical child. It is thought that children with ADHD produce fewer neurotransmitters, called dopamine, in the frontal lobe of the brain. These neurotransmitters are the "mailmen" of the brain in that they send messages to the different brain cells. If the brain has fewer of these "mailmen," it will consequently be less active. This means that the ADHD child is more susceptible to boredom and has fewer controls over internal impulses. Stimulant medication such as Ritalin is thought to stimulate the production of more of these "mailmen" (i.e., dopamine), and this results in a correction of the child's chemical imbalance.

Proponents of medication argue that children with ADHD need medication. They compare the child to a person with high blood pressure or diabetes, who also takes medication to correct a biochemical imbalance.

The most common stimulant medication is Ritalin. It usually takes a half-hour for its effects to become noticeable, and it wears off between three and five hours after being taken. It is not addictive and has no lasting effect. A child will usually take a small dose of Ritalin two to three times a day. I like to see a child start off with the smallest dose possible (typically five milligrams), and slowly work up to stronger doses if needed. This makes it less likely that a child will be overmedicated. A child who stops taking Ritalin reverts to the previous pattern of behavior.

Typically, the pediatrician, classroom teacher, or school

psychologist suggests that parents investigate the possibility of placing their child on stimulant medication.

The prescription of medication is a very emotional issue for parents. My philosophy here is to look at the advantages and disadvantages of the prescription of medication on a case by case basis. A review of the last twenty years of research indicates that if the proper dosage is prescribed, there do not appear to be any long-term side effects from taking stimulant medication. The most common possible side effects of stimulant medication are insomnia, decrease in appetite, headaches, and stomach troubles. Most of these side effects can be controlled by adjusting the dosage. A child who appears to be very tired or has uncharacteristic frequent mood changes is probably being overmedicated. Another potential side effect that used to be discussed in the research literature was a possible decline in physical growth rate. However, recent research indicates that stimulant medication has no real effect on growth potential.

A great advantage of stimulant medication is that it modifies the child's behavior inside and outside of the classroom. It may help the child to focus better on schoolwork and therefore achieve school success. It may also help to decrease the rate of inappropriate behaviors and therefore promote more positive interactions with peers, family members, and teachers. When used in conjunction with behavior modification strategies, it can be a powerful aid in improving a child's academic and social functioning.

One problem with stimulant medication use is that the teachers, parents, and physicians may not work together well to monitor the child's behavior effectively. It is extremely important that the physician who prescribes the medication gets feedback from all the significant adults who have contact with the child. This feedback is necessary to evaluate the medication and avoid possible side effects. I have often seen children placed on stimulant medication with no mechanism for feedback unless it is started by school personnel, such as the classroom teacher, school nurse, or school psychologist. The parent of a child with ADHD must monitor the child's adjustment to stimulant medication. This can be done through the use of the Medication Feedback Questionnaire offered in Chapter Four.

Another disadvantage to prescribing stimulant medication

is that it takes away internal control of a child's behavior and gives it to an external agent (i.e., the medication). When children with ADHD behave inappropriately, they often blame it on their lack of medication for that day or on not having enough medication. The use of medication also leads some parents to fear that their children will be more likely to experiment with illegal drugs. However, I have not seen any research indicating that this fear is justified.

The administration of stimulant medication will continue to be an emotional and controversial issue. My initial reaction is to first attempt extensive behavioral modification, teacher consultation, and psychological consultation. If all attempts at remediation fail, and the child is doing poorly in all areas, it may be beneficial to explore the use of medication. However, medication should be typically combined with other efforts to produce the best results.

The diagnosis of ADHD is still an inexact and subjective process. It is important to get information regarding the child's health, home, and school experiences. Sometimes the presence of ADHD is associated with other disorders such as oppositional defiance, anxiety, depression, obsessive compulsiveness, or Tourett's. Therefore, get a comprehensive assessment if you suspect your child has ADHD.

## *Emotional Problems*

Many children may be unsuccessful in school because of emotional difficulties. These emotional difficulties can be the result of negative early family interactions or stressful events. A lot of research focuses on the child's early social relationships with parents and how they set the stage for the child's relationships with peers, which develop later. The origin of the child's self-esteem and emotional stability, according to noted developmental psychologist Erik Erikson, is in early parental interactions.

However, when investigating emotional difficulties, one should look at the nature of both the child and the environment he or she has been exposed to. Each individual has personality and temperamental characteristics that interact with and help to structure the person's environment. For example, the child who has extreme characteristics of ADHD is very difficult for a parent to manage. This child does not respond to a parent's attempts to reason with him or her and never seems to own up to actions. The child is constantly getting into the same kinds of difficulties and doesn't seem to learn from mistakes. Moreover, the parents feel that they have little control over the situation. This kind of child is more likely to experience rejection and possible physical abuse within a family than a child who is calm and compliant.

Emotional difficulties can impede a child's academic progress by affecting the ability to tolerate frustration and deal effectively with anxiety in the classroom. Most academic learning involves some anxiety when new concepts are introduced. Typically, the child will rearrange prior concepts to integrate the new information, and this alleviates the anxiety. However, the child with emotional difficulties may be too anxious to attempt to rearrange established concepts. Instead, the child deals with the anxiety that results from the introduction of a new learning situation by attempting to withdraw from it. This withdrawal can be a passive withdrawal, or it may take the form of aggressive and distracting behavior. Children who exhibit overt acting-out behaviors such as hitting, talking in class, stealing, using obscenities, or being disrespectful are more likely to draw the attention of educators than those who are withdrawn or depressed.

Learning and emotional difficulties are often closely related. For example, it may be difficult to say whether a child acts out in the classroom and has a poor self-image because of emotional problems, or because of inability to complete the schoolwork successfully. It's like the old question of which comes first, the chicken or the egg. Some children, especially adolescents, may reject the school situation because such rejection lets them avoid dealing with the issues surrounding their lack of academic success.

Many children with learning problems continue to experience difficulties when they leave school at three o'clock. The negative impact of failure in school on their self-image can affect their performance in nonacademic activities. It's a similar situation to the man or woman who has a lousy day at the office. We would expect that lousy day to have an impact on how the person deals with other people. Could you imagine what it would be like if every day were a lousy day at the office? You would never be able to get your work done, and your boss would be disappointed. You would look at your coworkers who seem to handle the work with ease and wonder what was wrong with you. It would be very difficult to come home in a good mood and feel good about yourself. Expect a child with learning problems to be angry frequently and often to feel negative—that is likely how you would feel if you were unsuccessful every day at work.

Many factors could be involved in a child's lack of progress in school. Parents can take an active role in attempting to understand the specific elements that interfere with their child's progress. An informed parent is aware of the nature of a child's academic difficulties and is capable of having productive meetings with school personnel. An informed parent is also one who is able to question school policies that may be ineffective in promoting academic success. Informed and actively involved parents tend to be successful in getting positive educational results for their children. Information concerning the nature of academic difficulties is also useful in planning successful prevention and intervention programs. Chapter Two will provide you with information concerning the intervention programs that schools typically employ for children with learning problems.

# Things You Can Do

## EXERCISES

**1.** Attempt to get information on why your child has a learning problem. Investigate all the possible components involved in the learning process. For example, find out if there is a breakdown in:

- Paying attention.
- Familiarity with the content to be learned.
- Intellectual ability.
- Motivation to complete assignments.
- Task persistence.
- Ability to deal effectively with anxiety.
- Physical ability to complete a task.

**2.** Contact all the specialists involved in the diagnosis and treatment of your child's learning problem. You should contact the child's classroom teacher, special area teacher (i.e., reading, math, speech, special education), the school psychologist, and your child's pediatrician.

**3.** Talk to your child about the learning difficulties that he or she experiences in the classroom. You should realize that these difficulties impact on the child's emotional state and self-confidence outside the classroom.

**4.** Pretend that you are in your child's shoes. Imagine what it would be like to be unable to succeed in school. You could think back to when you were a child or make an analogy to your current job situation. You could imagine situations in which you don't understand how to complete tasks that most people are easily successful with. This exercise will increase your ability to empathize and to understand your child's learning problems.

**5.** Get a second opinion by consulting with a private psychologist or educator associated with a university learning center.

## QUESTIONS TO ASK YOURSELF

**1.** Is your child being presented with academic assignments that are developmentally appropriate?

**2.** Does everybody have the same expectations for your child's academic performance? Are those expectations realistic?

**3.** Has your child had a complete physical exam?

**4.** What positive educational experiences are you providing for your child at home?

**5.** How much individual attention is your child receiving to deal with the learning problem?

---

# 2

# PUBLIC SCHOOL INTERVENTIONS

## *Their Effectiveness and How Parents Can Best Take Advantage of Them*

■ ■ ■

*After being told that her son Johnny was "Learning Disabled," Mrs. Davis was informed by her son's classroom teacher that the school had wonderful services that Johnny was eligible for. Johnny's teacher said that he would now get the help that he really needs. Mrs. Davis asked Johnny's teacher what made her believe that these were the services Johnny needed. The teacher replied that she had heard that they were very good from other teachers. Mrs. Davis then asked if the teacher had ever visited the place in which these services were given or if she had read any research on these services. Johnny's teacher said no.*

## ACADEMIC SUPPORT SERVICES

The formal academic support services provided by public school systems can be divided into two types; special education and remedial services. To obtain special education services, a child must be referred to a Committee on Special Education (CSE). Some form of this committee exists in all school systems nationwide. The source of the referral could be the parent, teacher, physician, nurse, or other related educational specialist. The CSE is a committee that decides if your child has a "handicapping condition" that interferes with the child's "ability to learn." This committee may consist of a school psychologist, school administrator, teacher (typically a special education teacher), parent of a special education student, and a school nurse. Once a referral is made, the CSE usually has thirty school days to set up a meeting to determine if a child qualifies for a special educational service. During this time, the psychologist must complete a psycho-educational evaluation. Information concerning the child and the family background may be obtained by the school social worker, and a current physical examination will be requested. If the child has not recently had an evaluation by a pediatrician, the school may arrange for its own physician to conduct a brief examination.

To obtain a special education service from the CSE, a child must be labeled with a handicapping condition. The labels that are provided to children typically include "Learning Disabled," "Emotionally Handicapped," "Speech Impaired," "Mentally Retarded," "Hard of Hearing," "Visually Impaired," "Orthopedically Impaired," "Other Health Impaired," or "Multiply Handicapped." In my experience the most commonly used labels are Speech Impaired, Learning Disabled, and Emotionally Handicapped. The label is the price a parent must pay for a child to obtain a service. However, the label can be removed if the child makes sufficient academic progress in future school years. This is often the case for Speech Impaired children, but rarely the case for those who are classified as Learning Disabled or Emotionally Handicapped.

You have many rights as a parent in this process. The school psychologist will not meet with a child without parental permission. The CSE almost never labels a child without parental permission. If the CSE wants to label a child without such permission, it would have to take the parent to an independent hearing, which would cost the school district money in legal expenses. The committee would probably only take this action in circumstances in which the child presents significant behavioral and emotional difficulties.

If the CSE decides that a handicapping condition exists, your child would be recommended for various support services that range from full-time placement in a small class to periodic out-of-classroom support services. The CSE, by law, has to follow the principle of a least restrictive environment. Therefore, a child who can function in a regular classroom, should not be placed into a small self-contained classroom with other special education students. In addition, a child with a mild learning difficulty should not receive extensive out-of-classroom support services.

## GETTING CLASSIFIED BY THE COMMITTEE ON SPECIAL EDUCATION

The classification process is generally a very subjective one. The CSE committee reviews the psychological test results and teacher reports to determine if the child fits into a prespecified handicapping condition.

To be classified as Mentally Retarded or Mentally Handicapped, a child must have significantly below average intellectual functioning as measured by a standardized intelligence test (typically IQ scores of 70 or less). In addition, the child must exhibit significant deficits in adaptive behavior skills in the natural environment. Adaptive behavior skills refer to situations such as dressing oneself, being able to follow directions to get to the grocery store, being able to fix a sandwich, or being able to have positive interactions with peers. These are skills that will allow the child to function appropriately in the home environment but do not necessarily relate to academic success in school. Adaptive behavior skills can be measured through observations and adaptive behavior scales. It is important to investigate a child's adaptive behaviors because many members of minority groups have been inappropriately classified as being Mentally Retarded simply on the basis of intelligence tests.

The implication of the label Mentally Retarded is that the child will always be lacking in the general reasoning skills needed to succeed in school. In my experience, this label has been used less frequently in recent years. It has an extremely negative social stigma attached to it. My impression is that children from school districts with a lot of low-income families are more likely to receive the label of Mentally Retarded than those in wealthier school districts. In general, the potential negative effects of this label appear to outweigh any potential advantages. Children with this label will be typically viewed as inferior to other people for the rest of their lives. If a child is truly "mentally retarded," it will be very obvious to the child's parents and the pediatrician before the child enters school. Fortunately, the term is being applied less in recent years.

An example of a child correctly classified as mentally retarded is a boy I will call Tom. He is a physically healthy and well-behaved eight-year-old child who attends a special education class with eleven other children. Tom did not start talking until he was four years old, and even after that, his use of language always sounded like that of a much younger child. He still has trouble dressing himself and is not completely toilet-trained. Tom is generally slow to react to things and has a lot of difficulty understanding what is said to him. He is forgetful and never seems to figure out things for himself. Tom is not reading and cannot recognize letters, numbers, shapes, or colors. He is unable to play with other children of his age and usually spends time with either his siblings or preschool children.

To be classified as having a Learning Disability, a child must exhibit a 50 percent discrepancy between intellectual and academic functioning. This is usually illustrated by a child who has average intellectual functioning as defined by an IQ score of about 100 on an intelligence test, and scores several years below grade level on an achievement test. However, many children with low average or slightly below average intellectual functioning (IQ scores of 80–90) are classified by CSEs as Learning Disabled in order to receive extra support services. Technically, these children do not meet the criteria for obtaining special educational services. They are typically referred to as children who have the potential to "fall through the cracks." These children are sometimes classified by the CSE because of the lack of alternative educational programs designed to fit their unique academic needs.

The label Learning Disabled does not have the stigma of the label Mentally Retarded. The Learning Disabled child is viewed as having average intellectual ability and the potential (even if it is small) for future success in school. However, the label does imply that the child is different from other children and has a condition that has some permanency to it. In general, the label Learning Disabled is favored by most educators and parents over Mentally Retarded or Emotionally Handicapped because it has fewer negative connotations.

Linda is an example of a child classified as Learning Disabled. Linda is eight years old and achieved all her developmental milestones at the correct times. She started walking and using single words at twelve months of age and spoke in sentences by age two. Linda seems to get along with other children and has many friends to play with. She seems to have a good vocabulary and has no difficulty expressing herself. She is creative and makes up interesting games when playing with other children. Unfortunately, she still has a lot of trouble sounding out words. It took her a long time to identify the letters of the alphabet, and her writing tends to be sloppy. She tries hard but doesn't do as well as her classmates in reading and writing.

To be classified as Emotionally Handicapped, a child must demonstrate an inability to learn that is due entirely to emotional factors that are relatively enduring. These difficulties should be noted in more than one setting and cannot be due to intellectual, physical, sensory, neurological, learning, or motivational issues. The child's ability to learn has to be impaired by well-developed emotional issues. As with the Learning Disability label, the child's intellectual functioning is in the average range and the development of academic skills is below average. It differs from the Learning Disability label in its presumed cause of the academic impairment. A Learning Disability is typically viewed as being due to a malfunction in how the brain perceives and integrates academic information. A child with an Emotional Handicap is viewed as having a normal brain, but is unable to concentrate and complete school assignments because of a high level of anxiety. After several years of not completing schoolwork, the child falls behind. The school psychologist and school social worker play a large role in determining whether a child has an Emotional Handicap. A child who exhibits severe behavior problems in a classroom but has grade level academic skills does not technically qualify for special educational services. However, this point is often ignored in order to remove children who exhibit severe behavioral difficulties from regular classes.

Peter is an example of a child classified as Emotionally Handicapped. Peter is eight years old and has little respect for adults in school. While he achieved all his developmental milestones at age-appropriate times, he has always been a behavior problem at home. He constantly gets into fights with his parents and other children. He has poor impulse control and wants everything right away. He has difficulty waiting his turn and will often yell at or even hit others when he becomes upset. Peter has a good vocabulary and seems to have days when he can do good schoolwork, but typically doesn't because he is either disinterested or upset about something that happened earlier. Peter is the child who gets noticed because he disturbs his teachers and classmates. His teachers have a vested interest in getting him labeled because it often results in getting him removed from their classroom.

Another common label is that of Speech Impaired. This is a label that typically applies to preschool or young elementary school-aged children who have problems in the areas of vocabulary, use of grammar, speech articulation, or general communication skills. To qualify for the label of Speech Impaired, these deficits have to interfere with the child's educational progress. Many children with speech impairments go on to be relabeled as Learning Disabled in later years because of the strong connection between reading and language skills. Many other children are declassified and grow out of their speech difficulties.

Other handicapping conditions such as Visually or Orthopedically Impaired are less frequently used. They usually refer to overt physical or sensory handicapping conditions that can affect a child's educational progress. Special educational extra support services are provided to these children to help them compensate for their physical disabilities.

## SELF-CONTAINED SPECIAL EDUCATION CLASSES

In principle, the idea of a small class size or extra support services sounds appealing. Many parents and teachers are happy when a child receives special educational support services. They feel that now the child will get the help that is truly needed. However, the research on special educational support services is not terribly encouraging. No research clearly demonstrates the effectiveness of special education. No evidence shows that special education classes lead to more long-term academic growth than regular education classes. In fact, some research indicates that children may make better long-term academic progress in the regular than in the special education classroom (Madden and Slavin 1989).

A special education class usually consists of twelve children with significant learning and possible emotional difficulties. They only have one another as models for behavior and therefore lack exposure to appropriate role models. In addition, it is unlikely that the child will receive extensive individual assistance in the class. More often than not, the class engages in group activities similar to those in the regular classroom, but at a more basic level. There are also limitations in the type of support the child can get. Special education teachers are trained to use behavior modification strategies, deal with emotional problems, and organize work activities, but are not trained to be reading specialists. If your child is placed into a special education class because of a reading problem, it is unlikely that he or she will taught by a teacher who specialized in reading problems.

Supporters of special educational services argue that they remove children from a situation in which they experience failure and provide them with a situation in which they can experience success. Teachers and parents feel that children will feel better about themselves if they avoid the frustrations inherent in the regular classroom. This argument relies on the premise that removing the child from the classroom removes the social and emotional stress that results from having learning difficulties. It assumes that children forget about their peers in the regular classroom who are succeeding at their grade level. Even if you change the location of the instruction, most children are still aware that they do not measure up to their peers. It is likely that their feelings of being different and inferior will be reinforced when they are separated from their peers. The self-contained special education program also promotes the segregation of these children from average students. This often restricts a child's social interactions to only other children who also experience significant learning or behavioral difficulties.

Until I read the research on special education and observed children's progress in special education classes, I tended to support children's placements in self-contained programs. I assumed that a smaller classroom would be more beneficial for the child. I also had a lot of pressure from classroom teachers and school principals to support these types of placements. As I began to question self-contained special education programs, I also began to experience a lot of hostility from classroom teachers. On one occasion, a fourth grade classroom teacher reacted negatively when I tried to convince her to reconsider her recommendation to place a girl into a self-contained special education program (remember that the decision to place a child is up to the CSE and not the classroom teacher).

The girl's name was Sara, and her main difficulty was concentrating on her schoolwork. She was disorganized and frequently made careless errors when attempting to read or complete math assignments. I conducted a psychological evaluation of Sara and found that in an individual testing situation she produced a significantly more advanced level of academic skills than she was demonstrating in the classroom. In an individual testing situation, she was able to avoid outside distractions, receive a lot of encouragement, and put her best effort into answering questions. When I reported the test results to the classroom teacher, she decided that the test was invalid and in a metaphorical way decided to shoot the messenger. Some teachers feel threatened when a child can score higher on a standardized test than they perform in the classroom. A teacher could feel that if the test scores are correct then the teacher is somehow failing to get the child to work up to his or her full potential. Getting children like Sara to work up to their "potential" is extremely difficult when considering the makeup of the average classroom with twenty-five students. In general, this teacher was one of the better teachers in her school. However, she appeared to feel threatened by test results that implied that she was getting less than the maximum potential out of a child.

When it came time to discuss the special class placement, I noted that Sara would probably achieve the same rate or an even better rate of academic progress if she was left in the regular educational program. I also observed that most children in a special education class make relatively slow academic progress. I then made the mistake of illustrating this point with some of her previous students who had been placed in special education. I reported that I had tested several of her ex-students three years after their special class placement and found minimal academic growth. The classroom teacher then proceeded to report back to these children's special education teacher that I had insulted his teaching ability (which I had considered to be very competent). Instead of having one teacher angry at me, I now had two. Though it was not my intention to insult the special education teacher, my perspective on self-contained special education classes, based upon my experiences with children and solid research, could be interpreted as insulting. However, that wasn't my opinion in this case or in general. There are many excellent special education teachers. A child's progress in a special education class could simply be hampered by the absence of good role models, high expectations, and intensive individualized assistance.

Eventually, Sara was placed in a special education class and continued at her previous rate of progress. She did not perform any worse, but she did not make any significant progress either. I have learned the hard way to avoid attempting to convince teachers to take alternative perspectives. If a teacher or any other person is not initially receptive to hearing an alternative point of view, it is unlikely that any further discussion will be useful. In fact, as this situation demonstrates, it may actually be harmful. By taking a strong stance with Sara's teacher, I had damaged what was previously an amicable relationship. If I could live the situation over again, I would not have engaged in a strong discussion with Sara's teacher, and instead would have been more forceful in my interactions with Sara's parents. Her parents had the power to veto the process and could have prevented her move to a special education classroom. I often find that I have more success in convincing parents about educational choices than I do teachers. Teachers rely on their intuitive judgment developed from their prior experiences to make educational decisions. Lorrie Shephard and Mary Lee Smith, experts on the issue of repeating grades, point out that teacher decisions regarding educational decisions are typically based on the use of intuition as opposed to educational research. A teacher's intuition is not always correct, and that is the very reason educational psychologists conduct research. In general, educational research like that on special education is either ignored or denigrated by a large proportion of teachers and educators—a serious issue that needs to be addressed in today's schools.

## SPECIAL EDUCATIONAL SUPPORT SERVICES

Special educational support services supplement a child's academic instruction. Most commonly, the child goes to another classroom (pull-out program) to work with a special education teacher in the presence of approximately four or five other students. The child usually receives this assistance on a daily basis for one to two hours. This assistance is commonly referred to as resource room support services. Resource room support services may provide minor academic benefits, but they do not typically result in significant gains. When significant success occurs, it is usually with children who have at least average intellectual ability and are experiencing mild emotional difficulties. Proponents of resource room services argue that it may be the only place in which children can get instruction at their below average academic levels. However, teaching children at their level may not be sufficient to ensure that they make significant academic progress. If the instruction is merely a variation of the type that children were earlier unsuccessful with, it may be unreasonable to expect children to make notable academic progress. The children in resource room programs usually have significant learning difficulties and have not responded to traditional teaching methods. They need creative learning approaches that could be used by either the classroom or resource room teacher. Proponents of resource room programs also argue that they allow children to receive extra attention. However, it is unlikely that children will receive the intensive individual type of attention that they need to make real improvement.

In evaluating the decision to partake of resource room services it is necessary to judge each child on an individual basis. In general, these programs will lead to only small gains in academic achievement. On this basis alone, it would have the support of many parents and teachers. Obviously, some improvement is better than none. However, there are some inherent disadvantages in making use of resource room support services. It may fragment a child's educational program. You now have two teachers responsible for the child's education who have different teaching styles and may not coordinate well with each other. Sometimes the responsibility of primary instruction is transferred to the resource room teacher. This is not the mandate of the resource room teacher, who is only supposed to provide supplemental assistance. Transitions between classrooms can also lead to a loss of instructional time. The labels that children receive in order to obtain resource room services may also lead teachers, parents, and the child to lower expectations for performance. There could also be a social stigma attached for receiving the service. Typically, this is not an issue at the elementary level, but could be a major concern at the secondary level.

Overall, the decision to use special educational services has to depend on the other resources available for a child. If the child has no other resources available, then special education could be an option. Special education is not viewed as a good option for parents who can effectively work with teachers and assist their child at home. Chapters Three and Four give you information for working with your child's teachers, and Chapters Five and Six give you information for working with your child at home. Keep in mind that special educational services will not typically change a deficient student into a capable one. Most children who receive special educational services continue to receive them for most of their school career.

In some situations, special educational programs are both beneficial and actively needed. Special educational services can be very useful for children with documented physical disabilities. For example, a teacher aide can be placed into a child's classroom to help a child compensate for physical handicaps. A child with severe sensory impairment may need an aide to explain instructions, read educational materials, or help with physical needs. Modifications in the educational program, such as untimed testing, or length of time spent in school could also be instituted.

Special educational services are often needed for children who experience significant behavioral difficulties. Unless the child's emotional and behavioral problems have impeded the ability to learn, the child would not qualify for special educational services. Therefore, a child with average academic skills and significant emotional or behavioral problems would not technically qualify for special educational services. However, this requirement is often overlooked in order to remove children with significant emotional and behavioral problems from a regular classroom. If the child has extreme behavioral difficulties that cannot be managed effectively by a good classroom teacher, it may be necessary for the child to be placed in a special education classroom. This is done for the well-being of the child, the other students, and the classroom teacher.

In summary, if a child's learning is the major concern, and the child's parents are effectively involved in the child's education, I do not recommend the use of special educational services. When parents are not actively involved in a child's educational program, the special education teacher may be able to play a role in increasing their participation. With a small class size or caseload, the special education teacher has more time to call parents and set up meetings with them. However, that is not to say that attempts at parent-teacher coordination cannot be instituted by classroom teachers or other school personnel.

It is important for parents and educators to evaluate the effectiveness of services being provided to children. More service does not necessarily translate into more learning. Teachers often assume that an extra service will significantly improve a child's educational program. They assume that if the child is eligible for a service, then it must be an appropriate one. Even if a child is "Mentally Retarded," there is no reason that he or she cannot participate in regular classroom activities. The child will be no worse off in academic terms for staying in a regular classroom and may experience social gains. However, such a child may make more demands on the skills of the classroom teacher. In this situation, parents have to be advocates for teacher-training programs.

## REMEDIAL OR CHAPTER I SERVICES

In addition to special education support services, many schools have remedial reading or remedial math support services. Children who test at around the twenty-fifth percentile

(75 percent of students scored higher) on a standardized achievement test are placed in a small group (approximately five children) and work with a trained reading or math teacher. In principle, remedial services should be effective. In practice, they are often ineffective because a child with significant learning problems needs extensive individual support services. Robert Slavin, a researcher on educational interventions at Johns Hopkins University, found that children receiving remedial services do not typically catch up to the levels of the average students in their class. However, Slavin also states that remedial students do appear to make more progress with remedial assistance than without it. The big problem is that remedial programs do not typically provide the extensive individualized types of assistance that are needed for significant progress.

## Comparison of Resource Room and Remedial Services

Neither resource room nor remedial programs are effective in significantly improving the academic skills of children with significant learning difficulties. However, children in remedial programs usually have a higher level of academic skills than those in a resource room program. Therefore, it is more likely to see a child graduate from a remedial than a resource room program. Children who are successful in remedial programs tend to be the youngest students and those who have slight delays that are easily correctable. I almost never see older children with significant academic delays catch up academically through the use of resource room programs.

Remedial and resource room programs are typically pull-out programs. The children are pulled out of their classroom in order to get the educational service. There is currently a movement called "inclusion," which is having an impact on the way educators think. The inclusion movement recommends teaching all children within the classroom. In other words, instead of a child leaving the classroom for resource room instruction, the resource room teacher would come to the child. In general, the available educational research indicates that it does not matter if you pull children out of class or provide assistance within the class. It is the quality and the individual level of the assistance that is critical. There is no research to indicate that in-class programs are more academically effective than pull-out programs. However there may be social gains for remaining in the classroom.

Both remedial and resource room programs involve the use of labels. However, the label of "being math" or "reading delayed" is much more descriptive than the labels involved with special education. They describe the situation as opposed to attempting to explain it. Children realize that any student getting a remedial service is below average in that skill area. However, they do not receive a label that implies a cause of their problems or has much potential for denigrating effects. As previously noted, the labels used for special education attempt to infer causality for a child's learning difficulties, but they don't actually accomplish this task. Therefore, the special education labels may deflect educators and parents from looking at important educational issues.

The labels involved in remedial services are much more relevant and applicable for children. If a child has a reading difficulty, it is more useful to refer to the child as reading impaired than as learning disabled. For example, "Learning Disabled" children are not learning disabled in all academic skill areas, but that is what the label implies. If labels are to be used, I suggest that they be the descriptive variety used with remedial services.

Another way in which resource and remedial room programs differ is that resource room children have individualized educational programs (IEPs). All children in special educational programs have formal, written IEPs that specify short- and long-term goals, educational services, and academic restrictions. In principle, the IEP is an effective educational tool. In practice, it can be additional paperwork that serves no useful function. In my experience, the IEP is either generated by a computer without any teacher input or is constructed by the CSE or resource room teacher with little input from the classroom teacher. To develop an effective IEP, all the child's teachers, and especially the classroom teacher, should be involved in its construction. It would also be useful to involve the child and the parents in developing the IEP. Typically, the school district develops the IEP and requires the parents to read and sign it at a later date. The IEP meetings between resource room teachers are turned into a formality as opposed to a process of constructing a unique program. Developing an effective IEP should not be a routine process. It requires a high level of expertise and time.

The principle of an IEP should be applied to all children who need one, whether they are receiving special class, resource room, remedial, or gifted services. I have often constructed "unofficial" IEPs for children who have learning difficulties. The development of a good IEP is a means of preventing a child from being labeled with a handicapping condition.

For example, in June a teacher referred a fourth grade student named Jason to the Committee on Special Education because of his below-average reading skills. It was the end of the school year, and a competent psychological evaluation had already been completed on this child. Instead of subjecting the child to additional and unnecessary testing, I set up a meeting between his current fourth grade teacher, the parents, the child, and the future fifth grade teacher in order to construct an IEP.

During this meeting, Jason's academic strengths and weaknesses were discussed. His fourth grade teacher also listed the learning strategies that had been either successful or unsuccessful for Jason during the school year. We developed a plan that focused on Jason's strengths, such as his good vocabulary and high motivation to succeed. We considered these strengths when targeting his specific areas of difficulties, such as sounding out words and completing his work assignments. Some of the recommendations from this meeting were:

- A teacher or fellow student would review all written directions for assignments with him so that it was clear that he could understand them.

- Jason would raise his hand more frequently to ask his teacher for assistance.

- Jason would be allowed to give oral instead of written reports. These reports would be audiotaped, and his mother would transcribe them on paper. Jason could then copy what was written down in order to practice his writing skills.

- Jason would tutor a first grade student in reading.

- Since Jason responded so well to visual cues, next year's teacher would use diagrams or pictures when explaining things to him.

- Jason's teacher and parents would significantly increase the amount of recognition and praise he received for his progress in reading.

- Jason's teachers would attempt to minimize the negative effect of his reading problems on his other academic subjects.

- Jason would read out loud to his parents a book of his own choosing for twenty minutes a day.

- Jason's parents would spend twenty minutes each day reviewing the skills he learned in the classroom.

- Jason and his parents would be invited to another meeting at the beginning of the next school year to monitor his achievement of these goals.

Long-term goals regarding the promotion of Jason's self-esteem and positive attitude toward reading were also discussed. His teachers were pleased with the conference and decided to drop the referral to the Committee on Special Education. They now had a plan that provided an alternative to a problematic situation. Teachers often feel the need to make a referral to the Committee on Special Education because they see no other alternatives. An effective IEP is one such alternative. However, it does require a lot of teacher-parent-child cooperation to make an IEP successful.

## SCHOOL INTERVENTIONS
## THAT MAY BE HARMFUL

The most common intervention for children who are experiencing academic difficulties is for them to repeat a grade. There is a widespread belief among teachers that most children experiencing academic difficulties would benefit from an additional year in a grade. In the elementary school grades, this belief is based on the assumption that the child needs "the gift of time" to mature. However, the maturation model that is used to support grade retentions has no support in the educational literature. Therefore, teachers who advocate retention do so on an intuitive basis as opposed to one that uses current research.

Many teachers believe that repeating a child with the same curriculum will turn the child into a capable student in the future. However, I have trouble understanding this logic. Why would one expect a child to be successful with the same type of educational program that he or she was earlier unsuccessful with? Many teachers like the concept of grade retention because they think that it will provide for classrooms that are more cohesive and homogeneous. In actuality, retentions create a wide range of ages in classrooms and may eventually increase the disparity of abilities in a classroom.

The educational research is quite clear on the fact that there are no benefits in the long term to having a child repeat a grade. There is no research to support the use of retention to improve a child's long-term academic performance. On the other hand, a lot of research indicates that repeating one grade places a child at a higher risk for dropping out of school, and that repeating two grades almost ensures that a child will drop out (Holmes 1989). When children repeat kindergarten, they may look as if they're making progress when they enter first grade. However, when we look at these children in second or third grade, we see that they are one year older, but still at the bottom level of their class. There is no research that indicates that children have more self-esteem as a result of a retention. However, there is research that it leads to decreases in self-esteem (Shephard and Smith 1989). Retention is a traumatic experience for a child and one that the child will remember always. A child who is retained gets the message that something is wrong with him or her (i.e., the child is a failure).

Whenever I work with a child who has been retained a year, I explore every possibility of accelerating the child up to the grade with his or her age mates. I rarely get administration or teacher approval for this procedure. However, I often get approval for accelerating a child who has repeated a grade in two previous situations. When children repeat two grades, they are two years older than their classmates and become high-risk candidates for dropping out of school. Many children are repeated a grade because of a lack of effort as opposed to a lack of ability. I simply do not understand why some educators believe that repeating such a child would make the child work harder during the next school year. If the object of the retention is to teach the child a lesson, the lesson will be that the child is a failure. I have rarely seen a child work harder in school as a result of a retention; in fact, the opposite usually occurs. While the threat of a retention may motivate some children to put more effort into school, the reality is that retention usually results in lower motivation.

Adam is an example of a child who benefited greatly from acceleration to a higher grade. Adam transferred into a school I was working in as an eight-and-a-half-year-old first grader. His previous school had him repeat kindergarten and first grade. His teachers reported that Adam was immature and needed more time before he moved on to a higher grade level. While in kindergarten and first grade, he experienced the death of close members of his family and a parental divorce. Given the family difficulties at home, it was expected that he would experience some difficulties concentrating on his work in school.

When he entered first grade at the school where I worked, he was below average in reading. I volunteered to evaluate Adam because of his age, and I found that his reading difficulties were not significant and that he had average intellectual skills for a child of his age. I recommended that he be promoted to a second grade classroom. His first grade teacher was initially opposed to this idea, and she was the only person who had the authority to recommend acceleration. She was an excellent first grade teacher, who probably relished the idea of teaching this child basic reading skills. Some teachers do not like to move children out of their classrooms because they welcome the challenge of teaching a child with deficient skills. Elementary school teachers also tend to be overprotective of children and want to avoid placing them in situations in which they will be overmatched. There is also the common fear that the upper-level teacher will complain about being presented with a child who lacks the skills needed to succeed in the typical grade curriculum.

However, I was able to convince Adam's teacher to move him up to the second grade. In this situation, I could present a strong argument to the classroom teacher because the school principal had made it clear that the decision rested with her. I reiterated this position with the classroom teacher and made it clear that while I felt strongly about my position, I had no authority to make the decision. The teacher felt secure in her authority, and I was not a threat to it. On the other hand, my argument forced her to consider my point of view because she now had the responsibility of the decision and wanted to make the correct one. After several weeks, it was decided to place the child in the second grade on a trial basis. This recommendation was a compromise. In general I do not like to accelerate children on a trial basis because sending them back down a grade level will only reinforce their negative self-image.

Adam went on to second grade and initially experienced a lot of difficulty with the academic program. However, he was highly motivated to succeed and made good progress by the end of the school year. He felt terrible about repeating two grades and was extremely happy to be in the second grade. He was promoted to third grade, where he made a very good adjustment. In fact, I asked his third grade teacher how he was doing, and she wondered why I had even asked about him. He was doing fine! He was a well-behaved student who was completing all his schoolwork. I am convinced that Adam would have experienced both behavior and academic difficulties in future years if he had not been accelerated a grade.

Another common practice related to retention is for parents to delay a child's entry into kindergarten to "give them a competitive edge." Older children in kindergarten do in fact score moderately higher on standardized achievement tests than younger children. However, by the time these children are in third grade, the advantage evaporates. The initial advantage does not become a long-term advantage. Missing that first year of school increases the age disparity of the average classroom and could lead to problems if the child questions why he or she is held out. The typical response is that the child needed to mature (a message children interpret as "Something is wrong with me"). There is always a youngest child in every classroom and there will always be parents who attempt to create an advantage for their child. However, in the long run this practice is ineffective. If parents want to give their child an advantage, the best procedure is to provide them with an enriched home learning environment and to take an effectively active role in their education.

Another problem with retention is that it may prevent parents and educators from looking at the effects of an inappropriate curriculum for a child. The policy of retention implies that it is the child who failed, but ignores the possibility that the curriculum presented to the child was a failure. Many kindergarten students are recommended for retention because they were unable to succeed at a curriculum that was developmentally inappropriate for them.

Tracking is another potentially negative educational intervention. Tracking refers to separating high-, average-, and low-functioning students from one another. Robert Slavin, the John Hopkins educational researcher mentioned earlier, reviewed the research in this area. He distinguishes between the tracking that occurs in a classroom and the tracking that occurs as a result of being placed into a different set of classes. Slavin does not report any negative academic effect to within-class tracking, such as breaking up a class into small instructional reading or math groups on the basis of ability. However, in such grouping arrangements, the lower-track students typically get less instruction time than the higher-track students. For example, a classroom teacher will frequently break up a class into high-, low-, and middle-reading groups. These groups usually consist of about five or six children and run for about twenty minutes. Each of these groups gets the same amount of time to work on reading. However, it is not fair for the lowest group to get the same amount of time for reading as the highest group. Children in the lowest group actually spend less instructional time on reading than the other groups, as they need more time to have directions explained, they read at a slower rate, and they need more individual assistance.

Tracking into different classes is often done in middle and high school settings. Children tracked into the average or above-average group are not harmed. However, those in lower tracks typically make less-than-expected academic progress. Low-track classes are generally viewed as having a negative impact on students' learning. A low track is similar in many ways to a self-contained special education class. The children lack good role models and have diminished expectations for performance. It is much easier for teachers to conduct classes that are tracked because they are more homogeneous and involve less preparation and accommodation to individual needs. Therefore, many teachers may prefer to use tracking. Unfortunately, they have a detrimental effect on those children who need the most assistance. Once a child is placed into a low-track program, it is unlikely that he or she will get out of it. In general, parents should try their best to avoid having their children placed into a low-track program. Initially, it may look as if the child is succeeding and the teachers are happy with the child's progress. However, in the long run the child would likely perform better in a class of mixed abilities.

The research on children placed in low tracks is consistent and alarming. Whenever studies have been done to compare the progress of children in low-track classes to equivalent students in mixed-ability classes, the latter always achieve better learning.

## ALTERNATIVES TO TRADITIONAL INTERVENTION PROGRAMS

Most of the formal packaged support services are ineffective in remediating a child's learning difficulties. Most of the effective interventions I have seen were the result of good teaching and not special educational or remedial programs. This good teaching can of course come from special education or remedial teachers, but it can also come from a classroom teacher and even from parents if they receive the proper guidance. Some exceptional teachers have the ability to put forth the effort needed to help a child with learning difficulties make progress.

Sometimes a child's learning difficulties are so extensive that remediation is not the main issue. Instead, parents and teachers need to focus on allowing the child to be a successful participant in the classroom. A child who lacks certain skills or abilities need not become an outcast and a failure. The focus of the individual education program can be on adapting the child's daily work assignments to promote better classroom participation. For example, assignments could be modified to a level the child can understand and succeed at. The most important words in directions or assignments could be underlined or highlighted to help the child identify the central items. The child could be instructed to ask the teacher or a classmate to explain these items. Some children are unsuccessful in school because they do not attend to or understand the central aspects of their assignments.

Cooperative learning situations could be instituted in the classroom in which children work in groups with their classmates. The class could be divided into groups of three who cooperate to complete assignments or discuss issues. Some children could be uncomfortable working in a group situation with others because it could expose their lack of skills. However, unless the child becomes an active part of the educational process, it will be very difficult for the child to improve skill levels. It is also important for teachers to provide cooperative learning activities that allow all the children to play a successful role in the learning activity. For example, a child whose skills are very deficient can be asked to be the note taker or checker of work completion. Cooperative learning activities allow children to complete assignments within their capability and receive help from other students in areas in which they can benefit from assistance. Cooperative learning situations are most effective when they combine individual accountability and group rewards. Not all children need to be segregated from the regular classroom. Many children achieve a higher level of overall academic performance if they are allowed to remain in the regular classroom than if they are removed to a special educational classroom.

Parent volunteers, older students, or capable classmates can also provide individualized assistance to students. Schools can create a tutoring club in which older students work with younger ones on a regular basis. Ideally, this club would be run by a teacher who coordinates the tutoring activities with the classroom teachers and trains the tutors how to motivate and work with their tutees.

Teachers need to provide opportunities for children to feel internal control over their ability to succeed in school. Teachers and parents can actively promote the involvement of children in setting up their own goals for academic achievement in the classroom. This goal setting can even be done with young elementary school children. A child who has input into the selection of the goal will have a personal investment in it and be motivated to achieve it. Giving children choices also helps to increase their intrinsic motivation to complete their schoolwork. A feeling of no control over the learning environment can be very detrimental for your child's learning.

Martin Seligman proposed the concept of "learned helplessness" to explain why laboratory animals would give up trying to escape from an aversive situation. At first, dogs in his experiment could escape an electric shock whenever they wanted to. Then the avenue of escape was blocked. There was nothing they could do to avoid the electric shock. After a period of time, they were again provided an avenue for escape, but chose not to use it even though it was available. The dogs had learned that no matter what they did previously, they could not escape from the shock. It is important to avoid having children with learning difficulties acquire "learned helplessness," which implies that nothing they can do will allow them to succeed in school. We need teaching strategies that promote a child's sense of control or mastery over academic progress. The alternative is a dependent child who lacks confidence in his or her ability to succeed in school. Such a child is unlikely to put forth their best effort into becoming successful because of a belief that such success is not possible.

Whatever program is instituted, the child must experience success in it. For example, if the child's skills are especially weak, recognition tasks as "Was George Washington or Richard Nixon the first president of the United States?" may be more useful than the usual production task that asks "Who was the first president of the United States?" Easy recognition tasks provide the child with a greater opportunity for success and may improve attitudes toward learning and self-image as a learner.

Grade levels in schools are more a metaphor than a reality. Just because a child is in the third grade, for example, does not mean that the child has third grade skills. No matter what new types of interventions are created, we will always have children who do not fit the norm for performance in a classroom. It is often difficult for teachers and parents to accept the fact that some children will be unable to complete the same work as most of their classmates. Some teachers may take the attitude that a child who falls significantly below the norm cannot learn in the regular classroom and therefore needs another learning situation (i.e., a special education classroom). This attitude deflects responsibility for teaching the child. It assumes that since the child does not have the skills to succeed at the curriculum that is taught, the child cannot succeed in the classroom. However, success is a relative term: When the child cannot succeed at the curriculum presented, modify the curriculum. It is a lot easier to modify the curriculum than the child. A teacher can always ensure the success of the child in a classroom if the curriculum is effectively modified. However, such modification is a time-consuming task for which most teachers are not well-trained. Customizing a curriculum for a child may also mean using materials that are teacher created or modified, instead of standard texts and workbooks.

Meeting the needs of children with learning difficulties is a difficult task for teachers in any classroom, let alone a large one. Teachers should realize that when they develop an individual educational program for this year's Johnny, many aspects of the program will also be useful for next year's Johnny. Individualizing or dealing effectively with the diversity of abilities in the classroom is not an easy task, and it appears to be the major challenge to today's teachers. However, unless attempts are made in this direction, it is unlikely that low-achieving students will be made to feel like capable participants in their classroom.

Another issue that educators need to explore is the lack of good vocational programs for students who are sixteen years of age or younger. Most school districts offer vocational programs in areas such as auto mechanics, carpentry, plumbing, electrical work, food services, nursing and health care, and hair cutting. However, these programs are only offered to students after they have reached the tenth grade. Middle schools typically offer only brief introductions to some of these areas. Unfortunately, many students who are in most need of exposure to good vocational programs drop out of high school before they can become eligible for them. Many late elementary or middle school children could benefit from being exposed to vocational skills. Not every child will acquire the academic skills and the motivation needed to succeed in a college program. Therefore, parents may want to expose their children to vocational skills that are of interest to them at preadolescent to adolescent ages. They might contact shop teachers in schools, friends, or professionals who have skills in these areas. The age-old concept of apprenticeships is an appealing proposition for providing children with skills that will prepare them for future occupations.

I'm not suggesting that vocational instruction supplant the traditional academic program. However, I am suggesting that children with significant learning difficulties be given an opportunity to demonstrate skills in areas in which they will experience success. The acquisition of vocational skills will also provide more options for the future to the child with significant learning difficulties.

## EMOTIONAL SUPPORT SERVICES

Many difficulties that children experience in school can be traced to an unstable home environment. Perhaps the greatest complaint of teachers is parents who are unable to coordinate with them in setting up an educational program. Teachers find it very difficult to help children with learning difficulties when their parents are unable to monitor their completion of homework assignments. Many parents are so involved in their own stresses that they have little time to focus on the academic or emotional needs of their children.

The school system has an expanded role in our society. Teachers just don't instruct, they are often asked to deal with the effects of broader social problems such as divorce, alcoholism, drug abuse, child abuse and neglect, and malnutrition. The school system may be the only group in society that attempts to deal with many of these social issues because they directly interfere with their prime directive of educating students. However, schools only deal with these issues after they have had a negative effect on the child.

A child dealing with issues surrounding an unstable home environment cannot realistically be expected to put full ability into the academic program. A child who has to worry about an emotionally unstable or abusive parent has more things to concentrate on than reading or math. In situations such as these, the school system often attempts to help families through social workers or school psychologists.

The goals of counseling vary for each individual child. For some children, the goal is to alleviate the emotional distress of a traumatic or ongoing event: a death in the family, divorce, constant parental fighting, child neglect, witnessing a parent abuse alcohol or drugs, physical injury, physical defects, or even a reaction to academic failure. Each of these events places extra stress in a child's life. However, each child will deal with this stress in a different way. For example, some children will deal effectively with the emotional issues surrounding these events, and others will need massive forms of assistance. We can't measure the extent and need for assistance solely by the nature of the stressful event. We have to look at the child's personality characteristics and resiliency. We also have to look at the support system available for that child within the family and the community. A child with many support systems will deal much more effectively with stressful situations.

Sometimes school psychologists or social workers engage in individual or group counseling with children who have experienced a stressful event. Before such counseling takes place, there has to be a determination that the child can benefit significantly from counseling. In other words, the child's level of anxiety has to be interfering with school performance, personal relationships, or sense of well-being.

Counseling can also be used to help change a child's behavior. Of course, the parents or the child's teacher seek this type of counseling on the child's behalf. Children who exhibit inappropriate behaviors do not generally ask for help in changing their behavior. In fact, children rarely refer themselves for counseling; usually an adult requests it for them. When focusing on behavior, the school psychologist or social worker will generally attempt to coordinate with the child's parents and teachers to help provide positive rewards for appropriate behaviors and negative consequences for inappropriate ones. The focus of the counseling is less on counselor-child verbal interactions and more on child-environment interactions.

Another goal of counseling might be to promote positive changes in a child's school or home environment. In the school environment, the child could be helped to develop more positive social interactions with both peers and teachers. Role-playing is an excellent activity for this type of counseling because it allows the child to experience another person's perspectives. For example, you could ask your child to pretend to be the classroom teacher and ask how it feels to have a student talk back. You could also ask the child to pretend to be the person with whom the child last engaged in an argument. This would allow the child to see the other side of the disagreement and suggest different ways of resolving it.

Counseling can be a means of increasing teacher-parent-child coordination. The counselor is often viewed as an objective party by both the classroom teacher and the parents. The counselor is therefore able to promote open communication between parents and teachers in a nonthreatening way.

To obtain counseling for a child, the parents need to contact the school psychologist, school social worker, or school guidance counselor. Parents may also need to fill out a written request for counseling services. These services will be strictly confidential. In addition, the parents will have the right to all information gathered by the counselors. However, when adolescents are involved, the parents may want to waive the right to some of this exclusive information and make the child aware of this. Such a waiver will help promote a sense of trust between the adolescent and the counselor. However, if the child threatens to do anything harmful to self or to another person, the counselor is legally obligated to inform the parents.

The time period for the counseling sessions is determined by the individual counselor. As a psychologist in a public school system, I always try to meet with the child and the parents on at least one or two occasions. However, if there are extensive problems that will involve a lengthy period of counseling sessions, I often refer the family to a family counseling agency or a private psychologist. Like most school psychologists, I simply do not have the time needed to engage in lengthy counseling sessions with children and their families.

Counseling is a generic term that refers to a service provided to individuals with emotional or behavioral needs. However, the types of counseling available vary greatly. Some counselors take a psychodynamic approach that focuses on the individual's feelings, some focus exclusively on children's behaviors, some focus on their cognitive thoughts, and others focus on the dynamics of family relationships. Other counselors prefer alternatives to these more traditional methods by using art, music, or dance therapy. These forms of counseling are particularly effective for younger children who may have difficulty expressing themselves verbally.

Counseling is not an automatic cure for deep emotional

problems. For counseling to be effective, the participants must be actively involved in the process and have the desire to change their situation. It's like the old joke about psychologists, "How many psychologists does it take to change a light bulb?" "Only one, but it has to want to change." Counseling by itself does not change the home situation, which the child may have little control over. The point here is that counseling will not be effective in making a significant impact on a child's school life unless the parents and other significant family members are also involved and motivated to improve the situation.

Schools can also provide emotional support services to children by training peers as informal counselors. A school professional can train more advanced children of the same age to teach effective social interactional skills and to model appropriate behaviors. Children may find it easier to confide problems to peers and may take comfort in the fact that they have gone through similar difficulties.

Schools can also provide emotional support for students through strong, warm, supportive, and organized teachers. If your child is experiencing emotional difficulties, ask the school principal to recommend this type of teacher. While every student benefits from having such a teacher, the child with emotional difficulties almost requires one. A warm and supportive teacher will make a child feel more accepted and help lower anxiety levels. Ideally, this kind of teacher speaks softly to the child, rarely yelling. The child respects such a teacher because the teacher respects the child, and treats the child as a special person. An organized teacher helps to make the child less anxious by making events in the classroom predictable. When situations in a classroom follow a familiar pattern, a child feels secure. The child does not have to worry about what has to be accomplished in the classroom and knows what will come next. The child is confident with classroom routines. A child who is unsure about the classroom routine and is left with a lot of free time can become anxious and may exhibit behavioral difficulties.

Schools can also serve as agents for referral to public agencies or private psychologists for emotional support services. Because school staff are frequently in a position to make such referrals, they may be able to recommend the individual who would be most helpful to you and your child. It never hurts to ask.

# Things You Can Do

## EXERCISES

**1.** Attempt to set up conferences with the classroom teacher, remedial teachers, school principal, and school psychologist to discuss your concerns.

**2.** Look for ways in which the classroom routine can be modified to accommodate the learning difficulties your child is experiencing. Discussing a modified curriculum may be one of your major objectives when meeting with school personnel.

**3.** Attempt to get the school personnel together to set up a "true" individualized educational program. Goals and objectives need to come from all the teachers involved with your child. In addition, you, and especially your child, should become active participants in this process.

**4.** Ask the school if you can observe your child in the classroom and in remedial classes.

**5.** If you are considering a special educational placement for your child, ask to visit one of the special education classes to observe the type of instruction that takes place.

## QUESTIONS TO ASK YOURSELF

**1.** If your child is receiving remedial services:

- How many children are in the group?

- What activities are they working on?

- What activities is your child missing in the regular classroom?

- Have you talked to the remedial teacher?

- How often do the remedial and classroom teachers meet to coordinate strategies?

- What is the typical progress rate of a child in the remedial program? How many children reach a point at which these services are no longer needed?

- How does your child feel about receiving remedial services?

**2.** If your child is referred to the Committee on Special Education:

- What is the success rate for graduating children out of special educational services in your school district?

- What label will be used to classify your child?

- Will the special educational service lead to significant academic progress?

- What are the alternatives to using a special educational program?

- What will happen if the child does not receive special educational services?

- How does your child feel about receiving special educational services?

**3.** What opportunities does your child have to work cooperatively with other children?

**4.** Is your child consistently placed in a low-track learning situation?

# 3.

# SCHOOL SUPPORT PERSONNEL

## *Making Use of Them*

■　■　■

*Mrs. Sands was very upset when she looked at her daughter Brenda's second grade report card. The teacher had recommended that Brenda repeat the second grade. Why didn't the teacher alert her earlier to Brenda's difficulties so that Mrs. Sands could have done more to help her? Mrs. Sands was very strongly against the idea of Brenda repeating the second grade. She herself repeated fifth grade and did not want her daughter to have the same negative experiences. She was ready to go straight to the school principal to complain about Brenda's teacher.*

A parent in Mrs. Sands's situation should explore all the options available to her. If she goes straight to the school principal, she may alienate her child's teacher. She may also alienate the school principal if the principal finds out that she made no effort to discuss the issue with the classroom teacher. The teacher is still in a position to give Mrs. Sands useful information regarding Brenda's academic difficulties. Unless Mrs. Sands talks to Brenda's teacher, she will be unable to determine why the teacher was so concerned about her lack of academic progress.

The main issue for Mrs. Sands is Brenda's education. Before attempting to evaluate her child's teacher and fight the teacher's recommendation, she needs to obtain information regarding Brenda's academic difficulties—information she can only get by meeting with Brenda's teacher. A parent in Mrs. Sands's position might pose the following questions to a classroom teacher:

- Why wasn't she notified earlier about Brenda's difficulties? Perhaps Brenda's difficulties didn't become noticeable to the teacher until the end of the school year. Perhaps these difficulties were due to health or family issues that the teacher was unaware of.

- What are the specific areas Brenda is weak in? If her daughter has academic difficulties, it is important that Mrs. Sands be aware of them so that she can try to give her extra help at home.

- Why was Brenda having so much difficulty in school?

- What suggestions does her teacher have for improving Brenda's academic deficits?

- What are the alternatives to Brenda repeating a grade? Mrs. Sands and the teacher could even discuss which teacher would be best for her during the next school year.

Mrs. Sands could try to imagine that she is Brenda's teacher and decide what goals she would have for her daughter. Chances are she would find out that the teacher sincerely wants Brenda to be successful and is making the recommendation she feels is best. Mrs. Sands would realize that Brenda's teacher is a human being just like herself and is capable of making mistakes even when her decisions appear to be in the best interests of the child.

In bringing up the issue of her child repeating a grade, Mrs. Sands could start off by saying that she is unhappy about the recommendation. It's okay to express your feelings. As long as Mrs. Sands expresses her anger by beginning with the word "I" as opposed to the word "you," it is unlikely that teacher will be anything but sympathetic. Saying "I was unhappy about the recommendation" is a lot less hostile than saying "You made me unhappy with your recommendation." Using the word "you" to express your anger will most likely put the teacher in a defensive position and could interfere with your quest for helping your daughter's education. Another good word to use is "we." Asking the teacher how "we" can help a child leads to cooperation and joint problem solving. This is very different than saying to a teacher, "What can you do to help my child?"

As it turned out, Mrs. Sands had a cooperative meeting with Brenda's teacher. She asked the teacher for specific information regarding her daughter's academic difficulties and found out that she had a lot of trouble completing her schoolwork. These difficulties became more noticeable as the work became more advanced later in the school year. Unfortunately, the teacher was unable to tell her why Brenda was having problems. Mrs. Sands told the teacher that she felt Brenda was intelligent, and she couldn't understand why she was having so much trouble. The teacher agreed and suggested that Brenda be referred to the school psychologist for a psycho-educational evaluation. Mrs. Sands anxiously waited for the school psychologist to test her daughter. In about three weeks, the school psychologist conducted the evaluation and found that Brenda exhibited strong signs of neurological impairment. Her daughter was then referred to a neurologist, who also confirmed the existence of the impairment.

Brenda was a bright child who experienced difficulty paying attention and remembering things. After the neurological impairment was made known to the teacher, the issue of grade retention was dropped. Brenda would have the same difficulty paying attention and remembering information no matter what grade she was placed in. In this extreme case, the psycho-educational and neurological evaluation made it clear that the teacher could not consider grade retention as a solution to the problem.

After the evaluation, Mrs. Sands, the classroom teacher, the school principal, and the school psychologist met. Mrs. Sands asked that Brenda also be present at the meeting, since she was the one experiencing the learning difficulties. Sometimes we forget to involve the person who is experiencing problems in the solutions. Mrs. Sands reminded us all of the importance of her daughter's presence—she would, after all, be the one to put the most effort into working toward the goals set during the meeting. Strategies were discussed for helping Brenda pay better attention to her schoolwork and her teacher explored ways of adjusting the type of assignments she received to make them easier to remember.

By coming in to talk to the classroom teacher, Mrs. Sands gained insight into her daughter's academic difficulties and was able to get help in designing a more individualized academic program for her. The teacher wanted Brenda to be successful and now felt more comfortable with her because she had a better understanding of her difficulties. She was more willing to make adjustments in Brenda's academic program because there was a clear explanation for the academic difficulties she was experiencing.

Discussing Brenda's academic difficulties was a very productive exercise. It allowed her teacher to suggest a referral to the school psychologist and led to a meeting with several educators to help plan a more individualized academic program.

The school system has several support personnel who are designed to coordinate with parental efforts. Whenever a parent asks for assistance from a member of a school's staff, the parent should specify the type and degree of assistance. You cannot simply say that your child has a problem and you want help. A vague cry for help will likely lead to a vague type of assistance. You have to clearly state the problem and what type of help you are looking for.

## THE CLASSROOM TEACHER

The first and most important school staff member to be discussed is the classroom teacher. Developing a good working relationship with teachers is in your child's best interest. Your child's teachers have at least a bachelor's degree in education and typically have a master's degree in an educational specialty. Classroom teachers have to manage approximately twenty-five children. How many parents would like to spend all day managing twenty-five children? Typically, spending all day with our own one or two children can exhaust the best of us. The nature of the classroom unit places limitations on what the classroom teacher can provide for a child who is experiencing learning difficulties.

Perhaps the biggest challenge for classroom teachers today is dealing with the diversity of skills and previously acquired knowledge of their students. Children in classrooms exhibit a wide variety of backgrounds, personalities, learning styles, intellectual abilities, and academic skills. In many classrooms, there is a three-year level spread in the students' academic skills.

In a class of twenty-five students, the teacher cannot individualize instruction for all the students who are not functioning at the typical or average skill level. The instruction is geared toward the child with average skills in the classroom because this strategy typically reaches the most children. The typical classroom instruction is simply not directed to children at the extremes (i.e., the gifted child or the one with learning difficulties). The child with learning difficulties may not be able to follow the typical classroom instructional program because it is not directed at him or her. Many classroom teachers become frustrated by their inability to service the needs of the child whose academic skills are significantly lower than those of other children. They view special educational services as the only viable alternative for instructing the child with significant learning difficulties. However, as previously suggested, special educational services do not tend to be a particularly effective alternative.

In general, teachers have not been trained in college or graduate schools in how to plan effectively for children with significant learning difficulties, but school districts can develop in-service programs for teachers to expose them to programs such as cooperative learning or peer tutoring. These are alternative programs for teaching children with learning problems that do not involve their removal from the regular classroom. As a parent, you may want to write to your school district's board of education suggesting that they spend money on these types of in-service programs. You also want to make sure that the school districts fully implement these programs. I often see school districts attempt to implement intervention programs but fail to provide enough money to train teachers effectively or to purchase materials necessary to implement the programs fully.

The constraints of the typical classroom limit what the classroom teacher can accomplish for a child with learning difficulties. Parents need to be aware of these limitations and think of ways to work with the teacher to better their child's education.

## *Close Communication With the Classroom Teacher*

The most effective intervention programs that I have witnessed at the public school level have involved the parents, the teachers, and the child working in close cooperation with one another. When a parent is actively involved with the classroom teacher, the child gets the message that learning is very important. Why else would the mother or father want to become so involved with their child's education? The child also understands the need to do the best work possible because the parents will find out otherwise. An informed parent is in the best position to help the child become successful in school.

The classroom teacher also benefits from coordinating with parents who can inform them about a child's interests or abilities and share successful interventions that previous teachers have used with their child. Parents can support the teacher's attempts to get a child to employ the best effort in school.

Some parents would like to work closely with their child's teachers but do not for several reasons. It requires significant time and effort for a parent to visit the school and have contact with the teachers on a regular basis. It also involves a commitment to monitor the child's efforts at home which can involve a battle of wills between parent and child. It's a big step for some parents to make, and one that often needs encouragement from school personnel.

Typically, the child's mother is most responsible for overseeing a child's education, though the father's involvement is an important factor in a child's educational progress. I have experienced extraordinary improvements in a child's academic performance on several occasions when I was able to get the father more involved. I remember one particular child named Bobby, a fourth grade student who had completed little of his schoolwork since first grade. His lack of effort led to the development of below-average skills. He was a behavior problem in the classroom, constantly throwing spitballs, hitting other children, and walking out of the classroom without the teacher's permission. He was a very tall, heavy, and muscular child who was probably stronger than half the teachers in the school. His previous teachers had spoken only to his mother, and no one had made any attempts to talk to his father.

When I made an appointment to talk to Bobby's father, he said, "Why hasn't anyone asked to speak to me before?" Bobby's father had a good point. He was unaware of the extent of

Bobby's difficulties in school due to communication problems within the family. As it turned out, he was very willing to get involved in his son's educational program.

Bobby's father was about six feet tall and weighed nearly 240 pounds. He was a physically imposing person who was capable of being very stern with his son. I asked him to come to Bobby's school every day at three o'clock for a week to check on his son's progress. If Bobby had misbehaved or had not completed all his work, he was required to spend a half-hour with his unhappy father. If he performed satisfactorily, he got to go home with his happy father. When Bobby knew that his father was coming to school, he immediately stopped being a behavior problem in the class and completed all his schoolwork. A daily behavior and work completion check sheet was sent to his father in the subsequent weeks to monitor Bobby's performance. In addition, his father came in once a week to talk with the classroom teacher. For the first time since first grade, Bobby made good progress in his academic subjects.

Bobby's father put a great deal of effort into monitoring his child's performance in school. Not every parent is capable of making the same effort. In this situation, Bobby's actions called for extensive efforts on the part of his father. If his father had not become involved with the school, Bobby certainly would have been recommended for placement in a special educational program with little hope of significant progress.

The experience with Bobby's father is a success story I like to tell, but typically mothers are more involved than fathers in children's educational issues. I have seen many successful situations driven by a mother's concern. I remember a first grade girl who was very inattentive, ignored school rules for classroom behavior, and demanded a lot of teacher attention. Diane came from an unstable home situation in which her mother abused drugs and often left her without supervision. However, her mother loved her and wanted to see her succeed in school. During the course of the school year, Diane's mother entered a drug rehabilitation program, and the school social worker convinced her to visit Diane's teacher on a daily basis. While Diane continued to experience some behavior and academic difficulties, she did learn to read and became a functioning member of the classroom. I viewed her and her mother as one of the school's success stories.

Sometimes the threat of increased parent involvement alone can improve a child's academic performance. A seventh grade boy named Donald attempted little schoolwork for the first half of the school year. One of his teachers requested my involvement to evaluate him for special educational services. I looked through his school records and found enough information to indicate that he was capable of completing the schoolwork. I then asked his parents to meet with me. During this meeting, I suggested that one of his parents be prepared to spend a day going to classes with him if he did not complete his schoolwork. His mother volunteered to spend time in the classroom if necessary because his father could not take time off from work. I then brought the child into the meeting and stated that unless he started to do his work, "his mommy" would be visiting his classes. Being an adolescent, Donald was concerned with how the other students viewed him and did not like the idea of his mother invading his territory. We pointed out that it would be embarrassing for him to have his mother attend classes with him. Donald understood that his mother was going to follow through with her threat, and on that same day, he started to complete all his classwork and homework. I also developed a checklist for his parents to monitor his work completion. It was important for his parents to get feedback on Donald's daily progress, because it is so easy for students to slip back into old, strongly embedded work patterns.

Sometimes parents have good reasons for not working with a child's teachers. Parents who themselves experienced learning difficulties may understandably have negative attitudes toward schools because their own school failed to provide them with a good and beneficial education. Those who have scars from this experience typically have a negative attitude toward the educational system and may not want to work with it. The danger is that a child who sees a parent exhibit a hostile attitude toward the school system may model this attitude and become a less effective student. Schools can defuse these negative attitudes by inviting parents to become active partners in developing the child's educational program. Most parents are valuable resources to educators. They can often prove intelligent critics and good analysts of interventions that aren't working.

## Suggestions for Coordinating With Classroom Teachers

**1.** *If your child is having difficulty with a particular skill area, it would be beneficial to:*

**a.** Have a well coordinated program that is continually reinforced by those who work with the child. All of the child's teachers and the parents should share knowledge concerning the child's academic performance. You can't assume that the classroom and remedial teacher are in frequent contact and are working closely together. If you are unsure about the level of coordination, ask the school to arrange a meeting with all the child's teachers to check the level of coordination or to increase it.

**b.** Develop a behavior modification program that involves daily feedback from your child's teachers. This could take the form of a simple checklist on a piece of paper with all the days of the week listed. If your child is not responsible enough to bring back this checklist, telephone or mail the list on a weekly basis. It would be useful for your child's progress in an activity such as reading in the classroom to be graphed on a chart. A copy of this chart denoting the child's progress should be sent home periodically.

Alternatively, one of the parents could visit the school once a week to be informed about the child's progress.

**c.** Encourage your child to monitor both success and behavior. Your child can note progress in various subject areas on a chart.

**d.** Ask the teacher to seat your child next to a capable student and encourage the child to use this student as a resource for help, but not for copying answers.

**e.** Ask to have your child tutor younger children who are experiencing learning difficulties in a similar skill area. The tutoring activity will help to reintroduce your child to the basic skills in a nonthreatening way. Providing your child an opportunity to teach material will also force the child to understand the material at a deeper level. In addition, tutoring can boost your child's self-esteem. If your child cannot tutor in a subject area that he or she finds difficult, then attempt it in one of their strength areas. The opportunity to tutor will change your child's perception from always being a recipient of help to being a provider of help.

**f.** Encourage your child to raise his or her hand when unfamiliar with instructions.

**2.** *If your child is unsuccessful in school because of a lack of motivation and work effort, try to:*

**a.** Make arrangements for one parent to visit the school every day for a week. A child who has a successful day goes home at the end of the day and is told how proud the parents are of their effort. A child who is unsuccessful stays after school until the work is completed. Asking your child to complete the work after school at home is usually ineffective in promoting classroom work completion. The home situation is too far removed from the classroom experience. In addition, your response is most effective when the consequences are immediate and directly related to the problem situation. The goal here is to get your child in the habit of working. When I have employed this strategy, it has been successful in the vast majority of cases. Children do not want to stay after school and usually do want to please their parents. This strategy also serves the purpose of getting the parents more directly involved in their child's academic program. Once the child is becoming successful, the parental visits can be phased out to once a week and then once a month. It is also important to continue monitoring the child's performance with daily checklists sent back and forth between the teacher and parents.

**b.** For an older elementary or middle school child, you can threaten to visit the classroom for a day. Here the threat may be more effective than the action. For children exhibiting behavioral and motivational problems, the idea of a parent being in the classroom may make them feel very uncomfortable. They may be concerned about how they will be viewed by their peers. A parent who visits an older child's classroom is invading the child's special separate territory. This strategy has the potential of being a quick and effective way of improving a child's performance in school.

**3.** *Get a measure of the type of performance that is expected for your child.*

Compare your child's expectations to yours and those of the teachers. It is important that the expectations be realistic. Sometimes difficulties can occur because the expectations are faulty, not because any learning issues are involved. If you feel that a classroom teacher's expectations are unrealistically high, you may want to consult other professionals in the field of education, such as another classroom teacher at the same grade level, a school psychologist, a school principal, or a college professor in the field of education.

**4.** *Discuss the situations that promote success or failure for your child with the classroom teacher.*

Find out which situations are conducive to learning and which ones aren't. The classroom teacher and you view the child in different contexts and may have unique information to share with each other.

**5.** *Secondary students will benefit from having one particular teacher to turn to at the end of the day. For example, this teacher could:*

   **a.** Help your child organize assignments.

   **b.** Supervise your child's understanding of the assignments.

   **c.** Discuss situations that are presenting difficulty for your child.

**6.** *In working with teachers, it is best to establish a relationship of mutual respect.*

You should work under the assumption that the teacher also wants to see your child succeed in school. You have that common goal. If there is a disagreement, it will generally relate to the specifics of how to achieve that goal. If you are having a personality or other related conflict with the teacher, it is best to first try to work out the difficulties through an informal meeting with the teacher.

## THE SCHOOL PRINCIPAL

The principal, who typically is responsible for running the school, has a master's or doctoral degree in educational administration, and wants to promote a cooperative situation with the teachers. The principal must also be sensitive to the needs of children and parents in the community. In fact, a principal should have many of the skills politicians use to keep their constituents happy. When you go to a principal with a complaint about a teacher, don't forget that the teacher is also one of the principal's constituents. Most principals will give your complaint a fair hearing, especially if other parents have made similar ones. In response, the principal will use persuasion to keep all the constituents satisfied.

However, if a principal is ineffective in persuading a teacher to change a classroom procedure, it is unlikely that your child's learning situation will change. In that case, you could ask to have your child assigned to a different classroom or school. If the principal rejects this idea, you could bring your request to the superintendent's office or the board of education. As the principal's boss, the superintendent could put pressure on the principal to reassign your child.

Sometimes the school principal can play an active role in a child's education. As the school's main authority figure, a principal can enhance a child's academic performance by taking a personal interest in the child. I have seen many children beaming after being called down to the principal's office to receive praise or acknowledgment for their improved work. When the principal takes an active interest in the child's education, the student often perceives that he or she must be an "important" person.

## THE SCHOOL PSYCHOLOGIST

The school psychologist is another resource available to you as a parent. It is often useful to get another professional perspective on your child's learning difficulties. People in this position typically have a master's or a doctoral degree. The discipline is one that attempts to bridge educational and clinical psychology. Educational psychology investigates how people learn, while clinical psychology focuses on the issues related to mental and behavioral disorders.

From the educational perspective, school psychologists evaluate students' academic progress and serve as educational consultants to classroom teachers and parents. They are professionals trained in developmental issues and as such have insight into what are appropriate and sometimes inappropriate educational practices. As an educational evaluator, the school psychologist may administer and interpret intelligence and achievement tests. They also have statistical and research skills that allow them to interpret test scores and suggest methods of observing and evaluating student progress. If the school psychologist tests your child, you will want more than just a report of test scores. You want the assessment to lead to the use of strategies or a plan of action for helping your child become more academically successful. The second half of Chapter Four includes a more in-depth discussion on how to obtain a good psycho-educational assessment.

From the clinical perspective, the school psychologist often conducts an assessment of a child's social and emotional functioning, often using projective tests such as family or figure drawings, self-concept scales, sentence completion tasks, or picture interpretation tasks. These projective tests are meant to supplement an emotional assessment; they do not have the reliability or dependability of achievement or intelligence tests. Results of these tests must be viewed with caution.

It is important to look at how the child functions in everyday life, and school psychologists often observe children in the classroom or other school-related environment. The school psychologist uses the principles of behavioral assessment to provide an objective report on how your child functions in the classroom. The classroom teacher may be unable to provide this kind of detailed assessment because he or she has to watch the twenty-four other children at the same time. School psychologists may also want to conduct an interview with one of the parents concerning the child's early medical history and relationships with others. This can provide useful information on the origin and history of a child's learning difficulties.

School psychologists are trained to do individual or group counseling when necessary, although they do not typically conduct psychotherapy with children. Counseling is an educational activity in which problems and alternative methods of handling situations are discussed. Psychotherapy is a more intensive activity that may go deeper into family issues and attempt to uncover the origin of emotional difficulties. With the high rate of divorce in our society, it is not unusual for a school psychologist to conduct counseling groups for children from divorced families.

The school psychologist is also a resource for referring children to community agencies for various types of counseling or support services such as Big Brothers/Big Sisters. However, because of the high caseload, the average school psychologist finds it difficult to meet with every parent or child who needs services. Typically, parental concerns have to relate to a child's educational progress in order to justify the school psychologist's involvement.

Before attempting to consult with your school psychologist, you need to formulate clearly the type of assistance you are seeking. You must talk to your child and the teachers to express your concerns clearly. You can contact the school psychologist by simply making a phone call or filling out a written referral. Be aware that the psychologist may have a large caseload, and it could take a while before your request for assistance is honored. To ensure a timely response, attempt to get the psychologist to provide a rough idea of when you will be contacted. If you don't get a response within this time frame, you may have to remind the psychologist that you are waiting for assistance. You should take an aggressive approach to asking for assistance.

If you feel that your child has significant learning difficulties, you could refer your child to a Committee on Special Education. This committee usually has to meet within thirty school days of your referral. This means that the psychological evaluation has to take place within this time frame.

## OTHER SCHOOL PROFESSIONALS

The **school social worker** has a master's degree in social work and is trained to work with children and families to resolve emotional issues that could interfere with children's academic progress. They typically conduct individual or group counseling with children and meet with parents. School social workers are required to conduct social histories (a record of the child's previous health, emotional, and family history) for children who are referred to a Committee on Special Education. They may be able to suggest different parenting strategies or methods of improving a child's emotional state.

School social workers and psychologists are both involved in catering to the child's emotional needs. It is sometimes difficult to distinguish between the roles they have in the school system. My impression is that school social workers are more aware of public or private services that can provide assistance to children and their families. They are generally better appraised of services for which a child could be eligible, such as Big Brothers/Big Sisters, YMCAs, public counseling agencies, services for alcoholics and their families, or countywide social services. As a group, they also have more training in dealing with family-related issues while school psychologists tend to be more assessment and academically oriented. However, many school social workers get on-the-job training and learn how to provide useful suggestions regarding interventions for a child's educational program, just as the school psychologist does.

The **school nurse** is another member of a school system who may have insight into a child's emotional and academic difficulties. Sometimes the school nurse becomes the child's major confidant in the school system. After all, the nurse is at the school on a regular basis and is always available to a child.

On the secondary level, schools have **guidance counselors** who can provide assistance regarding a child's educational program and emotional functioning. Guidance counselors typically have a master's degree in counseling psychology. They often detect problems and oversee their resolution. Because secondary students have many teachers, it is difficult to get feedback on a child's progress and to plan an intervention program. You need to have one person step in to coordinate the efforts of your child's teachers. Typically, this person is your child's guidance counselor. Guidance counselors are often the first line of intervention at the secondary level although they will usually consult with the school psychologist or school social worker when situations involve exceptional types of difficulties. They are the key figures involved in monitoring and coordinating educational services in the middle and high schools. It would be difficult to plan any effective in-school intervention without their assistance.

## CHILD STUDY TEAM MEETINGS

An alternative to meeting alone with the classroom teacher or a school principal is a meeting with several educators present. Some schools have committees or child study teams that meet to discuss children who are experiencing difficulties in school. You could ask your school principal to invite you to one of these meetings or to set up a meeting with educational support staff to discuss your concerns. Child study team meetings are trouble-shooting sessions in which alternative educational procedures or options for your child could be discussed.

When you attend one of these meetings, be well-informed about your child's academic difficulties and some of the options for treating them. Try to get feedback on your concerns from other educators outside your child's school. Find out which school personnel will attend this meeting and write down your questions for them. The more prepared you are for the meeting, the more likely you will be to obtain the results you want. You may also want to involve a friend or family member who has been through this before or whose judgment you trust to assist you in writing the questions or to attend the meeting with you. Another way to prepare is to discuss your concerns with someone at the state education department to determine what services or program alterations schools can or cannot provide. Showing school personnel that you have contact with the state education department will let them know that you are a person who needs to be taken seriously.

Because a variety of educators are involved, the child study team is a good place to get answers to your questions. For example, you could ask:

- Do I have the right to refuse a recommendation for my child to be placed in a special education program? You do have rights guaranteed by the your state education department to contest special educational placements that you disagree with.

- Will my child be forced to repeat a grade over my objections? Some schools give a parent the right to refuse a grade retention for their child.

- How can I get my child evaluated by a school psychologist?

- What extra support services are available at the school for my child?

## RESPONDING TO DIFFICULT EDUCATIONAL SITUATIONS

The following are several examples of situations in which teachers failed to assist a child with learning difficulties. Alternatives for acting within and outside the school system are explored.

### *Michael*

Michael was an eleven-year-old in fourth grade. Michael repeated first grade and was classified by the Committee on Special Education as "Learning Disabled" when he was in second grade. He attended a regular second grade classroom and received extra support services for one hour a day in the resource room. He began fourth grade with academic skills that were closer to the average second grader than to the average fourth grader.

Michael was a well-behaved student who came from a family with a modest income. He lived with his mother and father, neither of whom had a high school diploma. In September, he entered Mrs. Briggs's fourth grade classroom. Michael's academic skills were significantly lower than those of his classmates. Mrs. Briggs referred Michael back to the CSE for him to be considered for placement into a special educational class. She felt that she could not teach Michael and that he needed to go into another classroom. She felt that she was acting in his best interests because he would not receive any special instruction in her classroom. The CSE decided not to place Michael in a special educational class because his skills were not significantly different from other resource room students.

Michael spent the rest of the year in Mrs. Briggs's classroom. She made almost no attempt to involve him in the daily instruction of the class. Her attitude was that he did not belong in her class, and she felt some guilt that the school district did not have a better learning environment for him. Mrs. Briggs was a teacher with strong opinions and was not willing to listen to alternatives that would allow Michael to be a functioning member of the classroom. I attempted to discuss the possibility of using cooperative learning procedures, peer tutoring, and alteration of curriculum materials. Mrs. Briggs viewed these as unrealistic suggestions that required an inordinate amount of work to benefit just one child.

Mrs. Briggs did not realize that it was her mandate to be Michael's primary teacher. This was not an optional mandate that could be overlooked because his skill level was less than that of his classmates. A fourth grade teacher is not just responsible for educating students whose skills who are at a fourth grade level. A grade teacher is "*the* teacher" for all the students in his or her classroom. While this is the practical view of the situation, some teachers deny it or find ways to justify their choice not to become more involved.

Michael's mother did not challenge Mrs. Briggs because she did not want to fight with the school system, nor did she have confidence in her ability to win a battle with a teacher. She also wanted her son to remain in his school because it had a much better reputation than the one he had previously attended. The end result was that Michael remained in Mrs. Briggs's classroom and lost a year of instruction.

In this situation, Michael's mother should have contacted the school principal and expressed her concerns about the teacher's unwillingness to provide him with the semblance of an appropriate instructional program. She needed to arm herself with the proper knowledge to be taken seriously. Having the appropriate knowledge and asking the right questions are critical to getting positive results. Michael's mother should have contacted the school district's CSE, the state education department, the school psychologist, or other educational personnel to ask the following questions:

- What were Mrs. Briggs's teaching responsibilities?

- What would happen if Mrs. Briggs was in noncompliance with state educational guidelines?

- Would Mrs. Briggs be responsive to attempts by school officials to train her how to teach children like Michael?

- Are there existing programs or teachers available that could instruct Mrs. Briggs on how to teach Michael?

- Could Michael be moved into another classroom in which the teacher would attempt to instruct him?

Michael's mother could have come to a meeting with the principal to voice these questions. The principal would have been forced to respond to her. The principal would have been even more responsive if she took notes about the answers to her questions.

If Michael's family had the financial resources, she could have explored the issue of sending him to a private school.

The decision to send a child to a private school should not be based on appearances, feelings, or other subjective criteria. You need to write down questions and get answers about many of the issues discussed in this book, such as:

- How much individual attention is provided? Make sure you get a detailed answer. Don't accept a response like "We give it if it is needed."

- How many children are in the average classroom?

- What are the typical academic skill levels of the children in the classroom?

- How will teachers instruct my child if the child is at a different ability range?

- Do the teachers use cooperative learning? If the answer is yes, have them explain how it is used. It's a good idea to read a little about cooperative learning before posing this question.

- Will teachers modify instructional materials for my child?

- Do the teachers have experience instructing children with learning difficulties?

## *Lisa*

The next situation involves a first grade girl named Lisa who was a significant behavior problem in the classroom. She was constantly talking and hitting other students. She also failed to complete any of her schoolwork. Her teacher's response was to assign Lisa to a desk outside the classroom. She certainly didn't disturb the teacher or the other children from her desk in the hall, but obviously Lisa could not learn how to read or to behave better when left literally outside the classroom. This is an extreme example of a solution to the teacher's problem that was no help at all to the child.

I found it unbelievable that Lisa's mother did not complain about this inappropriate use of a time-out procedure. Lisa's mother was not very involved with her child's education, nor was she concerned about Lisa's daily placement outside the classroom. If she had complained, Lisa's teacher would have been forced to deal with her inside the classroom. The principal would have been responsive to a situation that was open for inspection by the whole school and clearly inappropriate.

Part of the problem with Lisa's situation was her mother's lack of interest in taking a more active role in her child's education. If she had complained, she would have learned that her help and coordination was needed to improve Lisa's behavior and academic performance. Be aware that when you make a complaint about educational practices involved in a school, it may lead you to take a more active role in your child's educational program—an effort well worth your time and energy.

Unfortunately, Lisa ended up with significant academic difficulties in school because of the lack of good home-school coordination. Positive parental involvement would have prevented Lisa from having an extremely negative experience in first grade.

## *Mark*

Mark was a second grade boy who never completed his schoolwork in a timely manner. Mark's teacher assigned all his incomplete work as homework. Mark was a well-behaved child who spent almost three hours a day after school completing his homework assignments. His parents explained their concerns to his classroom teacher, who responded that Mark was a well-behaved child about whom she had no major concerns. The parents neglected to mention that Mark was working three hours after school on his assignments and was very unhappy. What second grade child would not be unhappy with this situation?

Mark's parents then contacted me for help. I found that Mark had visual-motor difficulties that were possibly the result of an early childhood illness. These difficulties meant that he completed written assignments at a slow pace. I observed Mark in the classroom and noted that he was trying very hard to complete his work, but simply could not because he was unable to write quickly enough.

I set about creating an instructional program that could help Mark compensate for his visual-motor difficulties. I suggested to his classroom teacher the his assignments be cut in half and that he not take any extra work home. In addition, I arranged for him to be provided with testing on an untimed basis whenever possible.

Mark's teacher was very accommodating in adjusting his educational program. His parents, it turned out, had experienced difficulty with his teacher simply because they could not clearly articulate the problems Mark was having. In this situation, the move to get a psychological evaluation helped to more clearly define the nature of his writing difficulties and provided for input from the school psychologist in adjusting his academic program. There was in fact no conflict between the teacher and parents. Instead, there was a communication problem that was resolved by inviting a third party into the process.

Before becoming upset with a classroom teacher, rule out the possibility of miscommunication. The school psychologist can be a valuable resource for parents attempting to alleviate any possible miscommunication. By involving another educator, both the parents and the teacher have a third party to interpret statements that were expressed earlier but possibly misunderstood. In this case, the third party also allowed for extra input in planning an educational intervention.

It is important not to turn your disagreement with the school into a personal one. Once that happens, effective communication often ends, and it could become difficult to resolve your concerns satisfactorily. Furthermore, if you don't show respect for your child's teacher, it will send a bad message to your children. If you can be disrespectful to teachers, then why can't your child? By negotiating your disagreement with school personnel in a professional manner, you will be modeling positive social skills for your child as well as getting help for your child's specific problem.

# Things You Can Do

## EXERCISES

**1.** Look at your child's teacher as your partner and attempt to share information that could relate to your child's educational progress.

You want to establish a relationship of mutual respect with your child's teachers.

**2.** If you have a disagreement with a teacher at your child's school:

- Attempt to talk to other educators outside your school to determine if your complaints are legitimate.

- Try to work things out with the teacher in an informal and friendly manner.

- Try to role-play or imagine why the other person thinks differently from you. Getting a feel for the other person's perspective may help you conduct a positive dialogue.

- Analyze how you typically handle disagreements with people. Make sure that you do not make your disagreement a personal one. If this occurs, it could be your child who is the big loser.

**3.** Find out which colleges have graduate programs in education or educational psychology. You may find a professor in one of these programs willing to talk to you about your child's problems. You could also do some research in the school library. It is useful to read books or journal articles on issues related to your child's difficulties in school.

**4.** Establish opportunities for both parents to be in frequent contact with school personnel.

5. Talk to your spouse about your child's difficulties in school and make sure that you have developed a consistent and coordinated approach.

## QUESTIONS TO ASK YOURSELF

1. What expectations do you have of your child's teachers?

2. Have the teachers met these expectations? If not, why not?

3. Have you treated teachers with respect?

4. When was the last time you and your spouse had a private conference with your child's teacher?

5. Do you know what the typical school day is like for your child?

6. How much individual attention does your child receive while being instructed?

7. Precisely what do you want your child's teachers to be doing that they are not doing now?

# 4.

# GETTING THE INFORMATION YOU NEED

■ ■ ■

*Brian was getting a failing grade in math, and he did not want his parents to find out. He was hoping that he could turn things around before his report card came out.*

Parents usually get feedback on their child's progress in school in the form of a report card. It typically consists of letter or number grades for your child's progress in various academic subjects. It often includes space for teacher comments, but the space is rather limited. Furthermore, a report card is sent home only about four times a year. It could inform you that your child had a very unsuccessful two months without your being aware of it in the least. If your child has learning difficulties, waiting two months to get feedback on your child's progress is simply unacceptable.

With the best intentions, some teachers send weekly reports to parents on a child's progress. These weekly reports are designed to keep a parent informed of their child's general progress. They are essentially a means of informing a parent if their child has behaved and completed work assignments. Weekly reports typically do not provide an in-depth analysis of your child's difficulties. Another problem with weekly reports is that they depend on the teacher's ability to write an objective and clear report. Sometimes teachers are so involved and frustrated by a child's learning difficulties that they can't look at them objectively. This could lead a teacher to focus more on the negative aspects of a child's performance than on the positive ones. It may also encourage teachers to focus more on the amount of uncompleted work as opposed to the skills with which the child needs assistance.

Report cards and weekly progress reports are not designed to respond to the specific questions you may have regarding your child's progress. It is difficult to plan tutoring sessions with your child simply on the basis of a report card or a weekly report. They do not provide detailed and specific information on skills your child has trouble with, or why. The only way to get this kind of information is by meeting with your child's teachers and asking the right questions.

## HOW TO ASK THE RIGHT QUESTIONS

It is normal for parents to have unanswered questions about a child who is not succeeding in school. Sometimes questions go unanswered because it is difficult for parents to find the time to meet with their child's teachers. Other times, parents fail to ask questions because they find the school an intimidating place. Schools are often associated with images of authority in our society. When we went to school, we were conditioned to follow school rules and not to question a teacher's authority or decisions. Some parents are afraid of asking questions because they don't want to look "stupid." There are no "stupid" questions regarding your child's education. Every time you ask a question, the answer increases your knowledge about your child's educational program.

It is not a special privilege for parents to come to their child's school and ask questions concerning their child's education. Part of a teacher's professional responsibilities include meeting with parents who have concerns and attempting to answer their questions. Most teachers I know are very happy to meet with parents and work together in solving a child's problems.

### Step 1. Defining the Problem

The major difficulty that parents have in getting information from school personnel is that they don't begin by getting a clear and detailed understanding of the problems their child is experiencing. Some parents are so concerned and anxious that they rush to solve their child's problems before finding out exactly what they are. Unless the school, the parents, and the child agree on what the problem is, it will be difficult to have meaningful and useful discussions. How can you attempt to fix a problem when you don't exactly know what it is? If you have a water leak in your house, you call the plumber. It is not enough to tell the plumber that you have a water leak. The plumber will talk with you to get more information concerning the leak before going to work on it. The plumber will specifically ask you where the leak is coming from and how bad it is. The plumber needs to define the problem before going to work on it.

When attempting to define your child's problem, be sure to ask questions about any labels that are mentioned. Anytime you hear a term such as "learning disability" or "immaturity," get a teacher to describe the specific behaviors that are causing concern. You need to discuss the exact behaviors or skills that are interfering with your child's academic progress.

To help define the problem your child is exhibiting in school, ask the following questions:

- *What are the specific skills my child is having difficulty with?*

    If a teacher says that your child is having difficulty with reading, you need to pin the teacher down and find out what specific areas of reading are presenting difficulty.

- *In what circumstances does my child exhibit this difficulty?*

    You want to identify the situations in which your child experiences difficulty. For example, sometimes a child may read better alone than in a group. Some children pay better attention if they sit near the front of the room than if they sit in the back.

- *How often does my child exhibit this difficulty?*

    Knowing how often your child exhibits a problem gives you an idea of its seriousness and gives you a starting place from which to measure your child's progress.

- *How does my child compare to other students in the classroom concerning this particular difficulty?*

    Knowing how your child compares to classmates gives you an idea of the frustration your child is experiencing and how the teacher perceives the child's difficulties.

## Step 2. Refining the Problem

Once you have a general idea of your child's difficulties, you will need to ask more specific questions. Get as much information as you can on the exact details of your child's difficulties. Ask your child's teacher to slowly rephrase the explanation of your child's difficulties so that you can carefully analyze it. You could also ask additional questions to help you refine your understanding of you child's difficulty, such as:

- Can my child pay attention to oral and written directions presented in the class?

- Does my child have the ability to read and understand directions for task completion?

- What skills or information does my child need to succeed?

- Does my child appear to be motivated to solve academic tasks in the problem area?

- What types of assignments are exceptionally frustrating for my child?

- How does my child compare to children of the same age in emotional adjustment, level of self-esteem, and relationships with others?

## Step 3. The History of the Problem

It is important to know how long your child has experienced a problem and what has been done to try to solve it. You want to get the following information:

- *How long has your child had this problem?*
  This question gives you insight into the seriousness of your child's difficulties.

- *What strategies have the current teacher and past teachers used concerning this problem?*
  You want information concerning both successful and unsuccessful strategies. You need to know what

strategies your child responds to before you can develop an effective intervention program.

## Step 4. Planning the Intervention

Once you have a good understanding of the nature and history of your child's difficulties, you are ready to sit down and plan an effective intervention program. Certain questions that you can ask will stimulate your child's teachers or other educators to come up with effective learning strategies. Sometimes the challenge of a good question can help a person formulate new and creative ways for solving a problem. You want to pose questions that lead to concrete suggestions for improving your child's functioning in school. You could ask questions like:

- What can be done to help my child complete homework more effectively?

- What can be done to improve my child's progress in reading?

- How can I make my child more motivated to complete math assignments?

- What services are available in the school to improve my child's academic performance?

- Does my child have the skills needed to succeed in the current academic program? If not, can the program be adjusted to meet my child's needs?

- How can my child pay better attention to classroom instruction?

- What behavioral difficulties is my child exhibiting in school, and how can we eliminate them?

- Are my child's physical handicaps interfering with academic progress? If so, what suggestions do you have for decreasing their negative effect?

- I suspect that my child is emotionally upset about something. Can you determine if my perception is accurate, and if it is, can you provide suggestions for dealing with this situation?

## Step 5. Evaluating Interventions

You should prepare a list of questions that will allow you to monitor the interventions that you and the school set up. For example, you could ask:

- How will we know if my child is improving?
- Can we have a daily checklist go back and forth, so that we can measure my child's progress?
- When can we get together again to discuss my child's progress?

## USING QUESTIONNAIRES TO GET FEEDBACK

Questionnaires can be an effective means of coordinating information between school and parents. You often see questionnaires developed by schools for parents, but never see questionnaires developed for parents to use with school personnel. Therefore, I have constructed sample questionnaires for parents to collect information from the school system. You can use the questionnaires to help define your child's difficulties, obtain feedback from teachers, and improve teacher-parent-student coordination.

---

## Child Performance Questionnaire

The Child Performance Questionnaire is to be filled out by one of the child's teachers and is designed to help parents get useful feedback on their child's progress in school. Ideally, the information gathered on this questionnaire could serve as the basis for the development of an individualized educational program. If the Child Performance Questionnaire is filled out before a parent-teacher meeting, the discussions can focus on your child's academic performance and how this performance can be improved. It will also promote the coordination of efforts between the parents and the classroom teacher.

Most teachers have never been asked to provide this type of detailed information on a child and may be reluctant to fill out the questionnaire. If this is the case, you should write a letter to the child's teacher expressing the need for his or her useful input. The letter should be written in a friendly manner that expresses your desire to work together with the teacher. If the questionnaire has not been filled out after two weeks, you may want to contact the teacher in person and inquire if it was completed. If another ten days go by, set up a meeting with your child's teacher and other educators, such as the school principal and school psychologist. At this meeting you could ask the questions presented in the questionnaire and write the answers down yourself.

### CHILD PERFORMANCE QUESTIONNAIRE

Child's Name _____

Today's Date _____

Date of Birth _____

Grade _____

School _____

Teacher Filling Out Questionnaire _____

1. List the child's strength areas: _____

   _____

   _____

   _____


2. Which skills or strategies allow the child to be successful in these areas? _____

   _____

   _____

   _____

**3.** List the areas where the child is having difficulty: _____
_____
_____
_____

**4.** Look at the child's problem(s) and determine if any of the following apply:

| | Yes | No |
|---|---|---|
| • Can the child pay attention to directions that are presented in class? | ❏ | ❏ |
| • Does the child have the ability to read and understand directions for task completion? | ❏ | ❏ |
| • Does the child have the skills or information needed to succeed? | ❏ | ❏ |
| • Does the child use the best strategies in solving tasks in this area? | ❏ | ❏ |
| • Does the child appear to be motivated to solve academic tasks in this area? | ❏ | ❏ |
| • Is the child easily frustrated when working on tasks? | ❏ | ❏ |

**5.** What short-term expectations do you have for skill acquisition in the following areas? Please write in terms of specific academic skills as opposed to grade levels.

- Reading _____
- Spelling _____
- Mathematics _____

**6.** What strategies have you used to address these deficits? _____
_____
_____
_____

**7.** Which of these strategies were successful?_____
_____
_____
_____

**8.** Which of these strategies were unsuccessful?_____
_____
_____
_____

**9.** What activities does the child appear to be interested in?
_____
_____
_____

**10.** What activities does the child appear to dislike?_____
_____
_____
_____

**11.** How can the child's parents be of assistance to the classroom teacher in helping to improve the child's academic functioning?_____
_____
_____
_____

**12.** When is the best time for teacher-parent conferences to take place?_____
_____
_____
_____

---

## Daily Performance Questionnaire

The Daily Performance Questionnaire is a method of getting daily feedback on your child's school performance from the classroom teacher. It is useful for motivating, monitoring, and evaluating your child's performance. This questionnaire is a necessity for the poorly motivated student. With such students, parents need to actively monitor their child's performance, always focusing on the positive. If the child has a "bad day," it should be ignored, and the child should be encouraged to have a good next day. It's important to set realistic objectives for improvements. If the child only has one good day during the week, then the goal should be to have at least two good days during the following week. The idea here is to make the Daily Performance Questionnaire a means of allowing the child to bring positive feedback to parents. Poorly motivated or unsuccessful students already have enough experiences with negative feedback.

Some sample objectives have been provided on the following Daily Performance Questionnaire. I suggest that you create your own objectives after talking to the teachers and your child. Start with realistic objectives that your child has a good chance of achieving. For example, if your child is only completing 20 percent of schoolwork, your objective for the first week may be for the child to complete 50 percent of schoolwork. During the next few weeks, you should attempt to gradually increase the rate of work to be completed. It is important that you do not initially set the criterion for performance at too high a level. Impossible demands won't help improve your child's performance.

### DAILY PERFORMANCE QUESTIONNAIRE

Child's Name _____

Week of _____

Date of Birth _____

Grade _____

School _____

Teacher Filling Out Questionnaire _____

If the child exhibits satisfactory performance in an area, mark it with a check. If the child does not exhibit satisfactory performance, leave that area blank.

|  | Monday | Tuesday | Wednesday | Thursday | Friday |
|---|---|---|---|---|---|
| Classwork |  |  |  |  |  |
| School Behavior |  |  |  |  |  |
| Homework |  |  |  |  |  |

**Teacher Comments:** _____

_____

_____

_____

Parent Comments: _____
_____
_____
_____

---

## *Classroom Behavior Questionnaire*

The Classroom Behavior Questionnaire is an attempt to get more detailed information regarding a child's behaviors in the classroom It's relatively easy for teachers to complete and provides information on specific behaviors that might need improvement.

### CLASSROOM BEHAVIOR QUESTIONNAIRE

Child's Name _____
Today's Date _____
Date of Birth _____
Grade _____
School _____
Teacher Filling Out Questionnaire _____

*Note the approximate percentage of time that the child accomplishes the following objectives and report any concerns you may have.*

| Objectives | Percentage of time | Concerns |
|---|---|---|
| Completes classwork | | |
| Completes homework | | |
| Follows directions | | |
| Stays seated | | |
| Is motivated to complete work | | |
| Focuses on classwork | | |
| Organizes seat work | | |
| Remembers what is learned | | |

| Objectives | Percentage of time | Concerns |
|---|---|---|
| Exhibits alertness | | |
| Participates in class | | |
| Uses good handwriting | | |
| Raises hand before speaking | | |
| Follows teacher requests | | |
| Respects others' property | | |
| Respects others' feelings | | |
| Attends school | | |
| Seems physically healthy | | |
| Gets along with peers | | |

## Emotional Concerns Questionnaire

The Emotional Concerns Questionnaire is suggested for parents who have children experiencing emotional or behavioral difficulties in school. The classroom teacher is asked to fill it out to give you a better understanding of your child's problems. If your child is having emotional or behavioral difficulties, these are likely to have a negative impact on classroom performance. You may have to address the emotional issues before you address the learning problems.

### EMOTIONAL CONCERNS QUESTIONNAIRE

Child's Name _____

Today's Date _____

Date of Birth _____

Grade _____

School _____

Teacher Filling Out the Questionnaire _____

**1.** List your major concerns regarding the child's behavior.
_____
_____
_____

**2.** During what time of the day are these concerns most evident? _____
_____
_____
_____

**3.** Describe a recent situation in which the child exhibited an inappropriate behavior that most concerned you.

　a.　Define the behavior. _____
_____
_____

　b.　What happened just before the child exhibited the behavior? _____
_____
_____

　c.　How did the classmates react to it? _____
_____
_____

　d.　How did you react to it, and what were the consequences for exhibiting the behavior? _____
_____
_____

　e.　How did the child react to these consequences? _____
_____
_____

**4.** Describe conditions that make it more likely for the child to exhibit inappropriate behavior. _____
_____
_____

**5.** List strategies that have been effective in promoting positive behavior. _____

_____

_____

_____

**6.** List strategies that have not been effective in promoting positive behavior. _____

_____

_____

_____

**7.** List activities the child is interested in. _____

_____

_____

_____

**8.** How can this child's parents assist the classroom teacher in promoting more positive behavior in school?

_____

_____

_____

---

## *Medication Feedback Questionnaire*

The Medication Feedback Questionnaire is to be filled out by the classroom teacher to monitor any child who is receiving prescription medication for possible side effects. Parents cannot take it for granted that medicated children will be actively watched by school personnel. Even a teacher with the best intentions may monitor a child but neglect to give parents feedback on that child's adjustment to a prescription medication. The Medication Feedback Questionnaire presents teachers with the opportunity to comment separately on your child's performance during morning and afternoon classes. Sometimes children take different doses of prescription medications in the afternoon or react differently to a medication taken after lunch. This questionnaire is particularly useful for monitoring a child who is being prescribed Ritalin for Attention Deficit Hyperactivity Disorder.

This questionnaire is designed to provide feedback on the behavior and academic performance of any child who is currently being medicated. Both parents and teachers are asked to provide their opinions regarding the child's performance. A copy of this completed questionnaire should be provided to the pediatrician who is writing the prescription for medication.

### MEDICATION FEEDBACK QUESTIONNAIRE

Child's Name _____

Today's Date _____

Date of Birth _____

Grade _____

School _____

Person Filling Out the Questionnaire _____

*Directions: Note if the child has any of the following difficulties. Then mark down the numbers referring to a behavioral concern you have for the child on the relevant day.*

1. Appeared tired.
2. Was frequently out of assigned seat.
3. Cried a lot.
4. Had little appetite.
5. Did not complete class assignments.
6. Schoolwork was sloppy.
7. Did not pay attention to directions.
8. Was defiant.
9. Exhibited frequent mood changes.
10. Appeared to be very anxious.
11. Was easily distracted.
12. Talked a lot.
13. Lost belongings.
14. Exhibited motor or facial tics.
15. Appeared to be sad.
16. Exhibited stomachaches.
17. Exhibited headaches.
18. Exhibited temper tantrums.

Week of _____

| | Monday | Tuesday | Wednesday | Thursday | Friday |
|---|---|---|---|---|---|
| AM | | | | | |
| PM | | | | | |

Comments: _____
_____
_____

---

## *Teacher Coordination Sheet*

The Teacher Coordination Sheet is proposed as a method for getting a child's classroom and special area teachers to better coordinate their efforts. The classroom teacher is responsible for making sure that each of the special area teachers completes the designated areas. The child carries the Teacher Coordination Sheet from the classroom to the special areas on a daily basis.

Sometimes teachers work on the same topic in different ways, and this adds to the child's confusion. The Teacher Coordination Sheet is a means of getting feedback to all the people involved with teaching the child, including the parents.

### TEACHER COORDINATION SHEET

Child's Name _____
Week of _____
Date of Birth _____
Grade _____
School _____
Teacher Filling Out the Questionnaire _____

**1.** *Skills that were worked on this week:*

  a.  Classroom Teacher Response_____
_____
_____
_____

b. Resource Room Teacher Response_____
_____
_____
_____

c. Reading Teacher Response_____
_____
_____
_____

d. Other Teacher Response_____
_____
_____
_____

**2.** *Skills that need to be reinforced are:*

a. Classroom Teacher Response_____
_____
_____
_____

b. Resource Room Teacher Response_____
_____
_____
_____

c. Reading Teacher Response_____
_____
_____
_____

d. Other Teacher Response_____
_____
_____
_____

**3.** *A successful strategy was:*

a. Classroom Teacher Response_____
_____
_____
_____

b. Resource Room Teacher Response_____
_____
_____
_____

c. Reading Teacher Response_____

_____

_____

_____

d. Other Teacher Response_____

_____

_____

_____

**4.** General Comments:_____

_____

_____

_____

----

## Student Perceptions Questionnaire

The Student Perceptions Questionnaire is designed to get feedback from your child regarding feelings about academic problems. A child's perceptions and feelings are extremely important information that needs to be included when developing an educational intervention program. Many parents and teachers neglect to directly ask their children these types of questions. This questionnaire is for you to complete and keep for reference when discussing plans or progress with school personnel.

### STUDENT PERCEPTIONS QUESTIONNAIRE

These are questions that you can ask your child regarding performance in school.

**1.** Are you having any problems in school? _____

_____

_____

_____

**2.** When did you start having this problem?_____

_____

_____

_____

**3.** Why do you think you have this problem? _____

_____

_____

_____

**4.** What is the best way(s) a teacher can help you?_____

_____

_____

_____

**5.** How do you think I can help you?_____

_____

_____

_____

---

# GETTING A GOOD
# PSYCHO-EDUCATIONAL EVALUATION

A psycho-educational evaluation is needed if you are unable to get answers to your questions during meetings with your child's teachers. There is no guarantee that getting a psycho-educational evaluation will lead to an effective intervention program for your child, but it's often a good place to start. Most psycho-educational evaluations are performed to determine if children qualify for entrance into special educational programs and focus on obtaining test scores, as opposed to pinning down skills that need to be improved. However, as a parent you want more from a psycho-educational evaluation than simply test scores. A good psycho-educational evaluation needs to:

- Define the specific skills your child needs assistance with.

- Provide an understanding of why your child is experiencing difficulty.

- Give feedback on your child's strengths and weaknesses.

- Provide information concerning your child's style of solving problems.

- Give you concrete suggestions for helping your child inside and outside school.

## Contacting the School Psychologist

Almost all public and private schools in the United States have access to free services of a school psychologist. Call your child's school to find out the telephone number and work schedule of the school psychologist. Then call that office directly to discuss your concerns. Many school psychologists have a large caseload, and you may have to wait several weeks for the next available appointment. If the school psychologist is too busy to meet with you, you may need to contact a school psychologist with a private practice. You can ask the local school psychologist, the classroom teacher, your pediatrician, or your state education department to give you a reference. Getting a private psycho-educational evaluation can be expensive—typically between four hundred and six hundred dollars—so it's important to have a clear idea of what you expect from a private consultation, and how that information can help your child.

You can force your child's school psychologist to make an evaluation by saying that you suspect your child has an "educationally handicapping condition." Public Law 94–142 of the federal government mandates that schools provide free psycho-educational evaluations if a child is suspected of having a "handicapping condition." You have to contact your child's school and ask to fill out some paperwork to instigate this type of evaluation. While your child will be examined, be aware that the evaluation is designed to uncover an underlying handicapping condition (i.e., to label your child), and is not specifically designed to develop an intervention program. It's likely that initiating this process could also lead to the labeling of your child. Therefore you should consider the consequences very carefully before you choose to make this type of referral.

## *Requesting Psychological Services*

Just as you did with the classroom teacher, you should carefully consider what you expect from a school psychologist's examination. Most requests for psycho-educational evaluations simply state that a child is being referred because the child is below grade level in academic performance. If the school psychologist merely confirms that the child is below grade level in reading, how will this help the teacher, parent, or child? You want the school psychologist to provide you with concrete suggestions for getting your child to the point where he or she can read at least as well as classmates.

Spend some time thinking about how to phrase your request for assistance to a school psychologist. Conduct a conference with your child's teacher to help you refine your request before you submit it to the school psychologist. When you fill out a request for assistance from a school psychologist I suggest that you list important events in your child's health, school, and emotional history, whether the school's form asks for them, or not.

## *Assessment of Academic Skills*

Typically, your child's academic skills are assessed through standardized achievement tests. These tests are called standardized because they are given in the same way to every child who takes them. Scores on these tests are compared to those obtained by a representative group of children from a similar age or grade level. These scores are expressed in terms of percentiles and grade equivalents.

A percentile score tells you how your child ranks in comparison to other children taking this particular test. A score at the ninety-ninth percentile is at the top level (the child scored better than 99 percent of the test-taking group), while a score at the first percentile is at the bottom level. A score at the fiftieth percentile is exactly average.

The grade equivalents are often misunderstood by teachers and other educators. They are based on percentile scores. For example, a fourth grade child who scores at the fiftieth percentile for a reading test at the beginning of the school year gets a grade equivalent of 4.0. for reading. The child who obtains a score at the fiftieth percentile for a sixth grader gets a grade equivalent of 6.0. If the score is at the the fiftieth percentile for a second grader, the child gets a grade equivalent of 2.0. You can't say, however, that a fourth grade child who obtained a grade equivalent of 2.0 in reading reads exactly like the typical second grade child. This child may have much less confidence than the typical second grade child and have different strengths and weaknesses. For interpretation purposes, the percentile is a more accurate descriptor of your child's performance than the grade equivalent.

Standardized achievement tests are administered on an individual and a group basis. Individual standardized achievement tests can provide useful information for planning remedial intervention strategies, but they are most effective when one looks at more than just the score. The psychologist has to informally assess the skill levels and strategies that the student has acquired. In this case, the psychologist and not the test is the instrument of assessment.

The most widely respected individual achievement test among school psychologists is the Woodcock Johnson Tests of Achievement–Revised (WJ-R). Other commonly used individual achievement tests are the Wide Range Achievement Test–3rd Edition (WRAT-III) and Peabody Individual Achievement Test–Revised (PIAT-R).

Group standardized achievement tests are usually administered to a large group of students by classroom teachers. Group achievement tests have limitations in describing a child's specific areas of competence or deficiency. Unlike the individually administered achievement tests, they can't:

- Look at a child's style of solving problems.

- Adjust the types of questions a child receives.

- Allow the examiner to question the child regarding mistakes when they are occurring.

Group standardized achievement tests are administered because of the widespread belief that they make teachers accountable for children's education. This is a misplaced belief because it is not an objective method of assessing a teacher's performance. Children's scores on such tests may reflect the abilities they had before they entered their current teacher's classroom. A child's prior knowledge will determine what can be learned in school now and in the future. To evaluate a teacher's performance, we need to pretest and posttest students in a classroom and have a comparison group (i.e., control group) for evaluating test scores. Group test scores can measure how different schools compare in achievement level. They may even be used to describe the range of student abilities in a school district. Unfortunately, they will not lead to specific educational interventions needed to help children learn more effectively. Individual tests are preferred to group standardized tests for helping an individual child.

Test results on standardized achievement tests are described in terms of percentiles or grade equivalents, which only provide a measure of how a child compares to other children. They are not true indicators of skill acquisition. This type of information is simply not useful for instructional purposes. It is used primarily for grouping children, for example, to form advanced, average and low academic tracks. As I previously discussed, this can be detrimental to your child's learning.

Ideally, you want to have more than grade equivalents or percentile scores as indicators of your child's school performance. A beneficial educational assessment should serve as a diagnostic procedure in which your child's academic strengths and weaknesses, and styles of problem solving are explored. It should also include recommendations to help your child become more successful in school. Potentially, the most useful type of academic assessment is called curriculum-based assessment (CBA). In this type of assessment, the psychologist or teacher creates a test to determine if the child has met the educational goals for an academic curriculum. The assessment is directly related to the specific skills taught in your child's classroom. This makes it easier to relate the assessment to intervention programs in the classroom. The test results from curriculum-based assessment provide direct feedback to a classroom teacher on how effective particular teaching lessons were for the child.

Curriculum-based assessment is currently in the exploratory stage. Most school psychologists still use standardized achievement tests to assess academic functioning. However, standardized tests only assess skills that are generally related to the instruction a child receives in a particular classroom. As educators become increasingly aware of the need to directly relate assessment to the child's educational curriculum, you may see an increase in the use of curriculum-based assessment.

## Intelligence Tests

An assessment of intelligence typically investigates a child's verbal and nonverbal abilities. Specific abilities such as expressive vocabulary, conceptual reasoning, factual knowledge, short-term memory abilities, and various puzzle-solving tasks are tested. The skills measured on intelligence tests are very broad and general and would not be significantly improved through the use of review courses.

The most commonly used intelligence tests are the Wechsler Scales of Intelligence, Stanford-Binet Intelligence Scale Fourth Edition, or Kaufman Assessment Battery for Children. These are individually administered tests that last about one and a half hours. I find that most children actually enjoy taking them.

Intelligence tests are typically viewed as measures of a child's "potential" to succeed in school. They tend to be good predictors for school success. However, they can be criticized as measures of "intelligence." There is no consensus among psychologists on what intelligence is. It is a hypothetical construct that is employed by people to explain why one person is more successful or has more ability in an area than another.

Intelligence tests have been and are used to provide IQ test scores. An IQ score of 100 is average. A score of 115 is above average, and scores of 130 or more are significantly above average. A score of 130 is typically used for determining entrance into a gifted program. A score of 85 or less is below average, and one of 70 or less is significantly below average. While the use of the score provides a broad estimate of a child's capabilities, it may have little value for those who are attempting to teach the child. For instance, how will the classroom teacher change teaching strategies after finding out that a child has a low IQ score? It's possible this information will only serve to lower the teacher's expectations for the child. If the child has an IQ that is average (and most IQ scores are in the average range), it's questionable whether the information will have any impact on how a teacher instructs. Confirming that a child has a significantly above-average IQ score may on occasion be very beneficial. It may lead the child to develop a better self-image and raise the level of the child's performance expectations. It is also useful for identifying intellectually gifted children who can benefit from adjustments in their academic program, but this will only be a small sample of children.

After examining what intelligence tests really do, one has to ask, "Why are they used?" This is a question that should be asked of all psychological tests. Currently, the main purpose of IQ testing in the school system is to classify students for entrance into special education programs. There is a big difference between using a test for classification and using it for diagnostic purposes. Classification only serves to separate children into groups, while diagnosis helps to plan intervention programs. Unless the intelligence tests serve a diagnostic purpose, they have little to offer us.

Intelligence tests could serve as an adjunct to the assessment process, but they should not hold the most prominent place in it. In most psycho-educational evaluations, an intelligence test is part of the standard battery. School psychologists have been trained for decades to give the same types of standardized intelligence tests. When I first started administering these tests, I did not question their value or utility. Administering the tests was what I was trained to do, and that's what I did. However, as I gave increasingly more of these tests, I began to question their value for the classroom teacher and the parent. Nobody was doing anything different as a result of the test scores obtained. Questioning the utility of the tests I was administering made me more sensitive to the reasons for evaluating a child. I was not there merely to give a child a series of tests and report scores to teachers and parents. Today, I view my role as assisting the child's teachers and parents in the process of developing a plan to make the child more successful in school

## Getting Feedback From the School Psychologist

Immediately after your child is evaluated, talk to the psychologist to find out:

- When will the report be written?

- When can you have a copy of the report? Most parents don't know that they are entitled to a copy of the psycho-educational report. This is a right provided by federal legislation that is usually referred to as the Buckley Amendment or the Freedom of Information Act. Some psychologists don't like to release their reports to parents. You can contact your state education department if you experience difficulty getting a copy of the report you've requested. It's your right. If a psychologist is uncomfortable putting something in writing, or uncomfortable that a parent may see something in a written report, then that information should not be included.

- When will you be able to meet with the psychologist to go over the results of your child's evaluation?

- What recommendations will lead to concrete positive changes in your child's educational program?

- If a diagnosis is made, what behavioral evidence supports it? Make sure that terms and labels involved in a diagnosis are put in terms you understand.

If the school psychologist is unable to answer your questions, ask for other resources (i.e., a private psychologist or educational specialist) who may be able to help you. Some colleges have child study centers or clinics that could help you get some answers to your questions.

# Things You Can Do

## EXERCISES

1. Write down questions that you want to ask the classroom teacher or psychologist before attending a school conference.

2. Contact other educators or friends for help in developing your questions.

3. Use some of the questionnaires illustrated in this chapter.

## QUESTIONS TO ASK YOURSELF

1. Have you prepared a list of questions to ask educators at your child's school?

2. Now that you've met with the teacher, are you still unclear about issues involving your child's learning difficulties?

3. Does your child need to have a psycho-educational evaluation?

4. Has an intervention plan been developed to help your child?

# 5.

# TUTORING YOUR CHILD AT HOME

■ ■ ■

Tutoring can be a successful and enjoyable experience for both you and your child. However, it's one that requires careful preparation on your part. As with any activity, your level of success will be directly related to your level of preparation and effort. Your effort will clearly be rewarded when you see the beneficial results for your child. This chapter describes the tasks involved in setting up tutoring sessions and preparing your child for a successful experience.

## PROMOTING ENTHUSIASM AND SELF-ESTEEM

*"Way to go, Craig. Keep it up, we're so proud of you." Craig's mother and father voiced their encouragement enthusiastically and often. Craig's mother gave him a big hug, and his father rushed to get his camera so that he could take a picture.*

Craig was a year old and taking his first steps. His parents, like most, were very excited about his progress and didn't hesitate to share their enthusiasm with him. It would be wonderful if you could bring that same sense of excitement and enthusiasm whenever you are working with your child. As a child gets older and accomplishments are taken for granted, parents tend to forget to share their excitement. Everyone needs praise and encouragement—especially children struggling to overcome learning problems. Don't hesitate to make comments directly related to your child's progress. For example, if your child has just completed reading a short story, you could say, "Mary, I'm so proud of you. That was not an easy story to read, but you pronounced those words wonderfully." Try to avoid making general statements that don't directly mention your child's accomplishments. For example, I wouldn't recommend saying, "Mary, you're such a good girl" or "You're such a good reader." If you don't mention your child's specific actions (i.e., pronouncing the difficult words in the story) she may not believe in your praise.

Your enthusiasm is contagious and very important in getting your child excited about the learning process. It also affects how your child feels about the work and how much effort the child wants to put into it. Acknowledging accomplishments helps the child develop a good self-image and promotes academic progress. Think of a time when you were in school or at work and had just written an excellent report or had solved a difficult problem for a customer. How willing would you be to write another report or help that customer again if your efforts went unacknowledged?

Your child's level of self-esteem and self-image as a learner is strongly connected to performance in school. To develop your child's self-esteem, you should provide many opportunities for success. Arrange your child's daily routine so that it provides a large variety of such opportunities. Your child's successes could range from solving a puzzle, figuring out the meaning of a new word, completing an art project, knowing the name for a letter, or simply having a positive social interaction.

Many children are unsuccessful in school simply because they lack confidence in their abilities. Your child needs to have an "I can do it" versus an "I can't do it" attitude. Your child also has to feel that it's okay to guess and make mistakes. In my experience assessing children with learning difficulties, I find that many avoid attempts at guessing. These children have an insecure problem-solving style and are reluctant to take chances. By not guessing and taking chances, they miss out on important feedback for new skill acquisition. Feedback is an essential element in making academic progress. It allows your child the opportunity to test knowledge and correct mistakes. Many children are so afraid of making mistakes because of its impact on their self-image that they fall back on conservative and risk-free responses. It is easier for them to say, "I don't know how," or "I can't do it" than risk being exposed as a failure.

Gary took this "I can't" attitude to school. He was a child with above average intelligence and at least average academic skills. Yet he was a poor student with a C average. Whenever

Gary experienced difficulty with schoolwork, he would with-draw from it. He was a quiet and well-behaved child, and his teachers liked him. They had no idea that he had the ability to achieve grades higher than a *C*. Gary had an older brother who was an A student and always on the honor roll. Gary did not want to compete with his older brother and felt that it was better not to try than to risk trying and not be able to measure up to his older brother.

Changing this "I can't" attitude to an "I can" attitude is a challenge, but an achievable, realistic goal. Gary's parents brought him to me for an assessment because of his poor performance in school. I gave him an intelligence test that demonstrated to both Gary and his parents that he was in fact a very bright child. I helped Gary and his parents raise their expectations of his performance. I instructed his parents to provide Gary with more emotional support and to help him build his confidence. Soon Gary was producing B quality work, much to the surprise of his parents and teachers. What he needed was for those who loved him to believe in him.

Believing in your child and providing opportunities for suc-cessful experiences is a key element in creating the confi-dence to be a risk taker rather than a risk avoider. If the success does not happen in the academic realm, you should attempt to provide opportunities for it in other areas, such as sports, the arts, or social skills. You want to ensure that your child has the self-esteem needed to approach problem tasks in a confident manner.

## MOTIVATING YOUR CHILD

*Mrs. Bacon was trying to help her daughter Anna with her math work, but Anna was totally uninterested. Mrs. Bacon should have known better than to try to work with Anna when "The Simpsons" was on TV.*

Probably the major complaint I have from parents who at-tempt to work with their children is that the children are not interested in working with them. These parents assume that the situation is hopeless but later find out that some minor changes can make the tutoring process much more enjoy-

able. First of all, you need to find out when is the best time
for you and your child to sit down and work together. Neither
you nor your child will be interested in working together if
either of you is tired or rushed. It is therefore important that
you actively get your child involved in setting the time, location, and length of the tutoring sessions. A child who has
some input will become a more willing and active participant
in the tutoring. Try to treat your child as a partner in deciding
on the conditions for the tutoring.

I suggest you have an open discussion about the need for
tutoring with your child. Instead of begging your child to work
with you, try to get your child to actively seek your assistance. After an open discussion about their academic difficulties, most children recognize the benefits that can be
achieved through working with their parents. In the unusual
event that your child insists that he or she does not want
to be tutored, I recommend that you explore the possibility of
involving a psychologist who could help establish guidelines
for a tutoring situation your child would agree to. The psychologist on staff at your child's school is a good person to start
with. Of course, you could also contact a private psychologist.
Your child's pediatrician could be a source for referrals.

Try to imagine what would motivate you if someone was
trying to help you with an activity that you have had a lot of
trouble with. You'd probably be very sensitive to criticism,
especially if it came from somebody you were very close to.
You would want somebody to be sensitive to your difficulties,
someone who would avoid comments like "You're wrong." You
would want a helper to focus heavily on the good things you
were doing and to be as gentle as possible when attempting
to correct your mistakes. You might even want the opportunity to correct your own mistakes whenever possible. You
would want your helper to respect you and treat you as a
competent person. This exactly describes how you should
treat your child.


## BEING PATIENT

*Mrs. Smith is upset because her daughter Jean has made
little progress in school during the last few years. Jean*

*has received resource room support services, remedial reading, and math help. Mrs. Smith doesn't understand why Jean is not making better academic progress.*

It's important for parents to realize that intervention programs usually involve slow and steady progress and require a lot of individual support to be effective. Be wary of people who promise tremendous acceleration in academic skills over a short time. Most academic gains are the result of good, intensive programs that provide maximum individual assistance. Mrs. Smith needs to find out exactly how much individual assistance Jean has been receiving in school. There is a big difference between receiving individual teacher instruction versus receiving instruction in a group with two or three other students. Most children feel more comfortable with and pay better attention to schoolwork when they have the undivided attention of an instructor. It is also easier for the instructor to attend better, provide increased feedback, motivate, and individualize instruction when working individually with a child. Tutoring your child at home is a way of significantly increasing the amount of that all-important individual academic assistance.

Having appropriate expectations for your child's progress is essential to providing calm and relaxed tutoring sessions. If your expectations are realistic, it will be easier to keep your patience when you are working with your child. You should also be aware of developmental issues involved in the learning process. Younger children require shorter sessions and have more difficulty paying attention to tasks. Younger children may also have inflated estimates of their capabilities and do not realize the amount of effort needed for them to complete a task sucessfully. They may have more difficulty in postponing immediate gratification, they are more impulsive, and they have less tolerance for frustration.

Make sure that both you and your child are enjoying the tutoring activity. If either one of you is unhappy, the session will likely be unsuccessful. Keep the sessions relatively short so that neither of you loses interest or becomes tired. Sometimes it is better to have three twenty-minute tutoring sessions than a single hour-long one.

## PREPARING TO BE A TUTOR

Once you have a willing participant, have established mutually acceptable times, and have some idea of how to motivate your child, the next step is to prepare yourself as a tutor. At this point, you may feel insecure about your abilities as a teacher. Don't dismay—remember, you were your child's first teacher and you have already taught your child many of life's important skills. While you may not have a teaching degree, you have a lot of teaching experience. You need not learn all there is to know about your child's academic curriculum. You only need to learn those parts the child is having difficulty with.

### Step 1

Obtain a diagnostic assessment of your child's abilities and interests. You need to know where your child needs extra help before you can plan an effective program. Try to set up a meeting with your child's classroom teacher to obtain the following information:

- *What are your child's strengths and weaknesses?*
  You want to get as much information as possible regarding your child's current overall skill levels, but especially in areas where the child has trouble. If your classroom teacher is unable to supply all the information you have requested, you may want to refer your child for a psycho-educational evaluation. This can be done by contacting the school psychologist or a psychologist in private practice. If you request a psycho-educational evaluation, make sure that you clearly specify to the school psychologist the type of information you are looking for.

- *At what level has your child acquired skills?*
  Are the skills at a surface or a deep level? Are they acquired at a hesitant or an automatic level? Sometimes a teacher or other educator thinks that a child has acquired a specific skill, but it later becomes evident that it is easily forgotten unless constantly practiced. For example, your child may appear to have

acquired the ability to multiply single-digit numbers in June, but when September arrives, the child has forgotten most of the multiplication facts. Perhaps the child did not have a deep and automatic recognition of the basic multiplication facts. Frequent errors or a long time to respond indicate areas in which your child has not acquired skills at an automatic level.

You want to attempt to reinforce and practice such skills by developing an instructional program that will focus on the speed of response. For example, you could explain to your child that you will be developing a game in which a correct answer to a multiplication fact earns one point and a quick correct answer scores two points. You want your child to practice getting the right answer within a short period of time if possible.

- *What is your child interested in?*
  Relating tutoring activities to your child's interests will make the learning task more appealing. We tend to pay better attention to and remember information if it is of interest to us. For example, if your child is interested in baseball, you could use baseball concepts in both reading and math-related skill-building activities. You could have your child read baseball stories to practice reading skills. Mathematical problems could be expressed in terms of team or individual statistics. Baseball averages are a good way to review the math concepts of averages and percentages.

## Step 2

Educate yourself in the skill areas your child finds difficult. Review your child's workbooks and textbooks. If you have questions, contact your child's teachers. Most parents have the skills needed to familiarize themselves with basic instruction at an elementary school level. Parents of children at a middle school level may have more difficulty with this task. It may also be necessary to spend extra time meeting with your child's teachers. Don't let this task daunt you. Remember, you don't need to be familiar with all curriculum areas, just the ones your child is having trouble with.

## Step 3

Set up instructional objectives or goals for you and your child. Allowing your child to have input into the type of goals being set will make the child an active contributor to the tutoring process and increase motivation. The goals should also be realistic ones that your child has a good chance of reaching.

In general, concrete and specific goals are more motivating than broad and vague goals. It is not enough to state that you want your child to read better. You must outline what specific behaviors or skills you want your child to exhibit after you start working together. I suggest you set up two types of objectives:

1. *General instructional objectives.*
   What are the general goals for your child? These are goals that broadly describe what you want your child to achieve but do not specify how you will measure your child's accomplishment of them. You could create general objectives such as comprehending the information in the classroom reading assignments, knowing basic addition facts, or knowing vowel sounds.

2. *Specific learning objectives.*
   Specific goals or objectives should be stated in the form of the specific behaviors you want your child to master. The following are examples of specific goals:

   • Add simple single-digit numbers without using fingers.

   • Summarize information in a short story.

   • Recognize appropriate sounds of letters.

   • Distinguish between the vowel sounds of "a" and "e."

   • Complete 90 percent of classroom assignments.

If your child is having difficulty recognizing letters of the alphabet, you could set up your goals in the following manner:

1. General instructional objective: My child will know all uppercase letters of the alphabet by the end of the school year.

2. Possible specific learning objectives:

- My child will recognize all uppercase letters by pointing at them when they are presented in a random manner.

- My child will correctly name the uppercase letters when they are presented in a random manner.

- My child will automatically (i.e., quickly) name all the uppercase letters when they are presented to her in a random manner.

## Step 4

Develop good communication skills with your child. You need to pay close attention to your child's feelings and be capable of reflecting them back to the child. It is important that you actively acknowledge your child's difficulties before you try to provide encouragement. For example:

- If your child's head is on the table, you can say, "It looks like you're tired now."

- If your child is starting to walk around the room, you can say, "I think it's time for a break."

- If your child becomes angry while working on a task, you can say, "This looks like a tough one."

- If your child is staring into space, you can say, "It looks like it's hard for you to concentrate right now."

Whenever facing a problem we can't solve, we don't want to hear that it is easy. We want affirmation that "Yes, it is a difficult task." If somebody tells you it is easy, and you can't solve it, the implication is "You must be stupid." Only after you verbally acknowledge your child's difficulties can you effectively provide encouragement.

Effective communicators avoid talking down to other people. You need to treat your child like a partner in the tutoring activities. Treat all the decisions in the tutoring process as issues to be jointly agreed upon.

## Step 5

Make a list of the strengths and weaknesses you will bring to the tutoring sessions. Don't just set goals for your child, set them for yourself. You may even want to involve your child in diagnosing your strengths and weaknesses as a tutor. Your child could give you feedback and help to make the tutoring process even smoother.

Set realistic goals for yourself in the tutoring sessions. If you have some initial difficulties, work together with your child and the teachers to improve them.

## GENERAL SUGGESTIONS

Before you attempt to tutor your child, you have to create conditions conducive to learning. You can help prepare your child for the learning activity by:

**1.** *Organize the tutoring materials.*

Having well-organized materials and a carefully planned lesson will increase the probability that your child will remember what is learned. Organization is one of the most important elements to effective learning. Your child could be experiencing academic difficulties in school because of a teacher's or school's disorganized curriculum. An organized learning environment is important but may not be enough for your child. Some children take a very disorganized approach to the learning process despite the best efforts of teachers or tutors to structure the learning activity. This type of child should practice getting started on and organizing work assignments that are similar to the ones received in school.

**2.** *Get your child excited about the learning activity by using visual imagery techniques.*

Ask your child to imagine pleasant or successful times previously experienced. You want your child to associate the tutoring with previous pleasant experiences. For example, if you are reading a story about the ocean, get your child to visualize a trip to the beach and how good it felt. If you are going over spelling words, ask your child to imagine what it felt like when the child received a good score on a spelling test.

**3.** *When giving directions to your child, attempt to establish eye contact.*

Having eye contact with your child increases the probability that the child's full attention is on what you say.

**4.** *Ask your child to imagine or mentally review the sequence of activities to be engaged in.*

A child who has a good idea of the sequence of activities will be more comfortable with the tutoring sessions. The child need not worry about what comes next and will be able to focus on the learning activities themselves. An outline of the learning activities that you will work on, step by step, may be helpful.

**5.** *Give your child practice in asking the right types of questions.*

Asking questions is conducive to acquiring new skills. Often students are judged by the types of questions they ask in the classroom. You may want to model good questions that relate to the topic you are working on.

For example, you could say, "I think that a good question concerning the meaning of the story is _____." You could then ask your child what another good question would be. You also want to train your child to ask questions when:

• The child doesn't understand how to complete a task.

• The child feels unconfident.

• The child is curious.

**6.** *Start off with relatively easy tasks to help your child build confidence and reduce anxiety.*

Once your child builds up confidence, you should present materials that are moderately discrepant from what the child already knows. If the information is too familiar, it may not be interesting, and if it is too challenging, it can provoke anxiety. Moderately discrepant information is motivating and interesting for children once they have confidence in their ability to succeed.

**7.** *Follow less pleasurable activities with more pleasurable ones.*

Vary the interest level of the activities. Mix in low-interest activities between high-interest activities. You could also present a format in which your child has to complete the low-interest activity before beginning the high-interest activity.

**8.** *Build novelty into your tutoring program.*

If you do the same thing every day, your child will become bored. Try using different modes for presenting information, such as through pictures or a chalkboard. You could also use different colored ink or paper on occasion. If you usually do your tutoring at the kitchen table, sometimes it's okay to do it outside or in your child's room. You could ask the advice of your child for ways in which the tutoring can be made more novel or exciting.

**9.** *Make sure your child experiences some success during instruction.*

If necessary, phrase questions as a recognition ("Is the answer X or Y?"), as opposed to recall ("What is the answer?"). Parents and teachers should also engage in the strategy of "shaping" desired behaviors. If your child cannot master a desired skill, you or the teacher should reinforce a behavior or skill that approximates the desired one. Parents and teachers can build on skills through successive approximations of the desired behaviors.

For example, when a child is having difficulty learning to write, you want to praise the child for writings that look remotely close to the desired letter. After a period of time, the child will make gradual improvements in writing the letters. You don't have to wait until the child writes a perfect "Q" before you offer praise. Initially, you could praise anything that looks like a circle. After a while, you could praise any type of line on the bottom or side. Eventually, the child will write something that closely resembles a "Q," and you will proudly acknowledge that it looks just like the letter "Q."

**10.** *Spend more time emphasizing your child's strengths than weaknesses.*

Remember that the child needs to feel confident about being able to be successful during the tutoring sessions.

**11.** *Phrase your feedback carefully and positively.*

Avoid situations in which you only provide negative feedback such as "You're wrong." Instead, take a positive approach in which you change the task perhaps several times so that your child can succeed with it. If it is not possible to restructure the task or your child cannot provide the correct response, then say in a nice way, "Try this," or "Say this." You always want to provide your child with the correct response in the least threatening way.

Examples of positive ways to note your child's progress include offering praise, using charts to mark progress, and prominently displaying nicely completed work.

**12.** *Focus on your child's progress no matter how small it is.*
Praise your child for progress as opposed to effort. Your child will not pay much attention to your praise unless the child makes progress in learning. It's like the baseball player who strikes out trying to hit the ball. The batter will ignore general comments such as "Nice try" or "Good effort." The batter needs to hear "your swing has improved, even if you don't get a hit."

**13.** *Maximize the time used during the tutoring sessions.*
It is not the amount of time that you spend with your child that counts. It is the amount of time that your child is effectively engaged in the learning activities that counts. Some children are remarkably adept at wasting time during learning situations. They get up to sharpen pencils, go to the bathroom, play with nearby objects, or talk about anything but the learning activities you are working on. Be aware that you may have to frequently guide your child back to the learning situation in a calm manner. Try not to yell. Yelling is an ineffective means of getting a child's cooperation. A nice calm voice setting up clear expectations and consequences for noncompliance is usually far more effective.

**14.** *Frequently drill and review skills that your child is acquiring.*
Try reviewing what your child accomplished during the previous tutoring session. This will help to clear up any misunderstandings that may have occurred and give both you and your child the confidence to move on to the next lesson. I also suggest that you have a brief review just before the end of each lesson. This will give

you and your child feedback on what was accomplished and help your child remember what has been learned.

## QUESTIONS YOU MAY HAVE

Once you have jointly agreed on clear objectives and have set up a plan for conducting the tutoring sessions, you may have the following questions:

**1.** How much should I involve my child in the planning activities?

Include your child as an active participant in the planning stages. Provide choices for activities whenever possible. Letting your child have input into the process will improve interest and motivation to participate in the tutoring sessions.

**2.** How serious an approach should I take?

Treat the tutoring as a fun activity and not as a chore that needs to be completed. Use humor and gamelike activities. Incorporating humor will increase your child's attention to the lesson and the probability of later recall. The sillier the lesson, the more likely your child will enjoy and remember it.

**3.** Where do I get educational materials to tutor my child?

Contact your child's teachers to get information for obtaining appropriate materials. Don't be afraid to modify them. Most textbooks or workbooks are designed for the child with average skills, and not for the child who is experiencing learning difficulties. You may want to use the school curriculum materials as general guides, but modify them to reflect your child's skills and interests.

You may also want to develop your own instructional materials. When doing this, consult the classroom teacher, school psychologist, or other educators. Making your own materials gives you the opportunity to be creative and develop lessons that are uniquely tailored to your child's interests and abilities. The instructional materials you develop need not be in written format. You could use multisensory approaches that involve video or audiotapes, pictures, and craft activities.

# Things You Can Do

## EXERCISES

**1.** Diagnose your strengths and weaknesses as a tutor. Use your strengths to build up the tutoring program.

**2.** Make a list of things you should and should not do when working with your child.

**3.** Read up on topics related to the skills your child needs to improve.

**4.** Practice setting realistic goals for your child. Share these goals with your child's teachers and other educators. You may have to revise these goals after receiving feedback from educators.

**5.** Don't forget that the tutoring can be a pleasurable activity for you and your child.

**6.** Be actively involved in your child's educational program.

- Talk to your child about the school day and take an active interest in what is being learned.

- Keep in contact with your child's teachers and attend parent-teacher conferences.

## QUESTIONS TO ASK YOURSELF

**1.** Is your child motivated to participate in the tutoring activity? If the answer is no, you need to have an open discussion with your child to encourage willing participation. Don't try to force the tutoring sessions on your child.

**2.** Do you feel positive about what you are doing? If the answer is no, you need to reevaluate your tutoring program and make adjustments.

**3.** Are you tutoring at the best time of day for both you and your child?

**4.** Can your child move on to the next level in the skill sequence?

**5.** Have you seen improvement in your child's performance in the classroom since you started the tutoring?

**6.** Does your child have a more positive attitude toward schoolwork?

**7.** Was your child allowed to have input into the tutoring process?

# 6.

# SPECIFIC TUTORING STRATEGIES

## ■ ■ ■

*This book has described a wide variety of learning problems, as well as the potential improvements children experience from individualized help. If you as a parent have decided to tutor your child at home, this chapter can be used as a resource for specific types of tutoring strategies.*

## RELAXATION EXERCISES

A child who is very anxious will probably need extra emotional support to put the best effort into schoolwork. Someone who is anxious can have difficulty concentrating and can become easily frustrated. Your child's anxiety can be lowered by these techniques:

**1.** *Use a soft, calm voice when speaking to your child.*
   Many times children attend to the form as opposed to the content of the message. Avoid yelling at your child because the end result will be the withdrawal of your child's attention.

**2.** *Try to acknowledge your child's feelings.*
   Don't say your child "has no right to feel that way." Instead, let your child know that you understand how he or she feels. Acknowledging your child's feelings promotes a healthy emotional relationship. The child feels secure in the knowledge that you understand. Sometimes children misbehave to get parents or teachers to acknowledge their feelings.

**3.** *Make the learning sessions predictable.*
   When we know what to expect, we usually have fewer worries or concerns.

**4.** *Use relaxation exercises in which your child tenses and gradually relaxes muscles.*

You and your child should find a comfortable place to sit and conduct your tutoring sessions. Before you start tutoring, develop a little relaxation ritual that the two of you can engage in. For example, you can spend a minute or two going through some breathing exercises:

- Take a deep breath and slowly let the air out through your nose.

- As you breathe in, slowly raise your hands until they are over your head. Stretch your hands as far as they can go. Hold your breath a second or two and then slowly let the air out while slowly lowering your hands. Repeat this activity once more.

- Now close your eyes and place your hands in your lap. Notice how effortlessly the air goes into and out of your lungs.

If during the tutoring sessions you notice that your child is squirming or becoming fidgety, you could try isometric exercises, which consist of tightening and relaxing various parts of your body. For example, you could stop the tutoring session for two minutes and do the following:

- While keeping the rest of your body relaxed, squeeze your fingers together to make a fist. Gradually squeeze tighter and tighter. Notice the tension and then let go. Let all your anger and frustration go. Focus on your hand and how relaxed it is.

- Now do the same thing with your other hand. Make a fist and gradually make it tighter. Feel the tension and let go of it. Notice how your hand feels when it is relaxed.

# TUTORING READING

Reading is an extremely important skill area because it is involved in almost all the academic assignments your child will have to complete. Most children referred to me have learning problems related to reading skills. Reading difficulties are extremely frustrating for children in elementary school because they are often asked to exhibit their deficiencies by reading out loud in front of other students. Middle and high school students may exhibit behavior problems to avoid bringing attention to their poor reading skills. It is less damaging for a child's self-image to be viewed as someone with a "behavior problem" than as someone who has a "learning problem."

You can improve your child's reading ability by using specific reading strategies. Keep in mind that the older the child you are working with, the longer the history of frustration and negative experiences. You want to do all you can to be sensitive to your child's feelings and take as positive an approach as you can.

The following are general suggestions for making your home a reading-friendly environment.

**1.** *Read to your child on a regular basis, starting at age one.*
   You may want to start this process even earlier if your child feels comfortable with it. A child who has been read to has the equivalent of thousands of hours of individual reading tutoring and develops a solid background from which to acquire reading skills. The child whose parents do not read to him or her starts off at a significant disadvantage. Listening to stories helps children see how language is segmented, builds vocabulary, serves as a model for reading, and lets the child know that reading is a pleasurable activity.

   When parents of young elementary children ask for advice for their child with reading difficulties, most educators stress the development of a positive parent-child reading program.

**2.** *Encourage your child to increase the amount of reading at home and decrease the amount of television time.*
   It would be nice for each family to have a set time in

the evening for reading activities. Children who see parents read are more likely to engage in independent reading.

**3.** *Try to be actively involved in your child's reading program.*
I strongly recommend weekly trips to the library with young school-aged children. Buying books at a bookstore can also be a special reward for your child. You want to impress on your child that reading is a valued activity.

The following are some specific suggestions for increasing your child's reading performance during the tutoring sessions.

**1.** *Reading lessons should be consistent with your child's ability to pay attention.*
If your child has difficulty sustaining concentration for long periods, it is better to offer several short reading tasks as opposed to a single long one.

**2.** *Take turns reading pages in a book with your child.*
This strategy is particularly effective for children who also have attending or motivational difficulties. These children are likely to read more pages in the long run if an adult sits with them and alternates reading pages. The anxiety that they experience is lowered and they have less difficulty following the contents of the story.

**3.** *At the beginning of each week, have your child pick five words that he or she finds difficult.*
Each of these words could be written on flash cards. Then the child could practice spelling the words and creating sentences that use them.

**4.** *Have your child trace his or her foot and make about five to ten copies.*
On each copy, have your child write a new word or letter. Tape the copies around the wall of your child's room. Have the child practice sounding them out while following a trail. You could also try to tape the words on the ceiling over your child's head. Try to use the most common or central words that create difficulty in everyday reading or in the classroom. Have the child practice these words until they have been learned at an auto-

matic level. Then rearrange their order on the wall to make sure that the child has learned the words as opposed to the word order.

**5.** *Tape record your child reading a sentence or short story.*
Every few weeks, compare the new reading to the old one. Praise any progress—and congratulate yourself too.

**6.** *Time how long it takes your child to read new words with a stopwatch.*
Children will respond to praise for correct pronunciation as well as for speed of performance.

**7.** *Reward your child (perhaps with a small coin) for sounding out each new word correctly.*
Keep a list of new words and of how much money the child has acquired.

**8.** *Have your child tell a short story while you write it down, and then have your child copy it.*
You can use this story to improve your child's writing and spelling skills. This can be done by emphasizing the new words to be learned in the child's own story.

**9.** *Encourage your child to write poems.*
Many children enjoy this activity. Encourage your child to use new words.

**10.** *Your child will need constant positive reinforcement to recognize words at an automatic level.*
Don't be concerned with providing too much positive feedback to your child. You can never go wrong by making your child feel good about accomplishments.

**11.** *Try to avoid sounding out words for your child if possible, and always give your child the opportunity to correct errors.*
Giving your child the opportunity to self-correct reading lets the child try out new skills and increases self-esteem. If you always correct the reading, you provide a lot of negative feedback. Who wants their mistakes to be constantly pointed out for them? By allowing your child the opportunity to find his or her own mistakes, you are encouraging a more confident and self-reliant reader.
If it's necessary to correct your child, try to offer part

of the word and ask the child to sound out the rest. You want to give every opportunity to exhibit reading skills.

**12.** *Expose your child to multisensory approaches to reading.*
For example, train the child to imagine the word printed on a page, then attempt to write the word on a piece of paper with his or her eyes closed. A blindfold may be useful for this activity. Have your child practice saying the word out loud while writing it down.

**13.** *Help your child use association strategies.*
You could develop flash cards with a picture on one side and the word on the other side. The sillier the picture is, the easier it will be to remember later. For example, for the word "block," you could ask your child to draw a block on top of somebody's head. Eventually you can fade out (not show) the picture, and ask the child to read the word.

## TUTORING MATHEMATICS

Preventing difficulties in math is extremely important. Once a child acquires a strong case of math phobia, it is difficult to overcome the fears. If your child is having slight difficulties with mathematics, do not wait for a crisis before intervening. This is especially true for adolescent girls, who are at greater risk for math phobias.

Before tutoring in math, you and your child should talk about how the child feels about math. Your most significant contribution may be to help the child feel more comfortable about engaging in math exercises. Let your child know that you understand how he or she feels about math. The child will be more willing to work with you if you understand how difficult it is. Try to build up your child's confidence in their abilities by starting with relatively easy examples and slowly working up to the more difficult ones. Always give your child the opportunity to reach the answer alone. There will be no sense of accomplishment if you provide the answer.

Mathematics is typically composed of organized and specific sequences of instruction. Before you start tutoring, you need to identify any gaps in your child's skills. Often a child is able to compensate for gaps up to a certain point, but when the difficulty increases, the child will begin to experience significant problems. Tutoring in mathematics should therefore be based on a thorough understanding of your child's skill levels. You need to have a conference with your child's teacher and find out what skills have been acquired. If you are still unclear where to start, you could seek out an educational specialist to perform a diagnostic math evaluation. If a remedial math specialist or school psychologist is unavailable in your child's school, you may have to contact a private psychologist.

Unless you know your child's weaknesses, it will be difficult for you to develop effective tutoring lessons. You need to find out the answers to the following questions:

**1.** *Can my child adequately read the math assignment?*

Sometimes difficulties in math are simply due to the child's inability to read the math assignments. If that is the case, someone needs to read them out loud.

**2.** *Does my child understand the various steps involved in solving a particular math task?*

If you can't break down the steps involved in solving a math task, ask your child's teacher to help you. You need to know which steps your child has mastered and which ones you need to help with.

**3.** *Does my child use the best strategy to solve a problem?*

Sometimes it's not enough to obtain the correct answer. For example, some children obtain the correct answer to addition problems by counting fingers. However, the counting method will not be adaptive when the time comes to multiply and divide. In the long run, it is best for your child to use more efficient strategies in solving arithmetic tasks. Most of the children whom I have seen experiencing math difficulties have been unable to develop automatic recognition for addition, subtraction, multiplication, or division. When asked to add "9 + 6," they count their fingers as opposed to automatically giving the correct response. This causes them to become very slow at calculating their answers and interferes with their acquisition of more advanced math skills. These children need to spend time memorizing basic math facts.

**4.** *Does my child have a pattern of making careless errors?*
   Some children understand how to solve various math assignments but make frequent mistakes because they either rush through their work or have difficulty sustaining their attention. This type of child already knows how to solve the math task and may not need further math instruction. Instead, the child may need assistance in slowing down and being more careful in checking work. For example, the child could be instructed to:

- Put a finger on the numbers that need to be computed.
- Check to make sure that the appropriate math operation is being performed (i.e., multiplying instead of adding).
- Review answers before handing in the assignment.

## BEHAVIOR MODIFICATION

If you suspect that your child's emotional difficulties are interfering with learning, you can use behavioral modification strategies that are applicable to most situations. For example, you could:

**1.** *Use positive reinforcement.*
   A child who is tense will need a lot of praise and encouragement while working on academic assignments. Try using one, two, or all of the following:

- Smiles.
- Verbal approval. "I like the way you're sitting in your chair." "I'm so pleased at how you're paying attention." "I'm so pleased by your performance."
- Points.
- Checkmarks.
- Hugs.
- Stickers.
- Use of preferred activities, such as playtime.
- Concrete physical rewards.

**2.** *Focus on the one specific behavior that interferes the most with academic performance.*

Don't try to focus on too many negative behaviors at the same time. Instead, focus on the activity that is most disruptive to the tutoring sessions.

**3.** *Provide immediate consequences (positive or negative) for your child's behaviors.*

Deal with the inappropriate or appropriate behavior immediately. The longer you wait, the less effective your message will be for your child.

**4.** *Illustrate your child's progress on a graph.*

If the graph is not illustrating progress, then the type of tutoring and the materials you have used need to be reevaluated. If the lessons are structured appropriately, there should always be progress. However, this progress may be incremental as opposed to radical. Try to complete a daily graph at the end of each learning lesson.

**5.** *Revise the type of positive reinforcement your child receives.*

After a time, the novelty of the reinforcement may wear off, and your child could return to previous levels of performance. This is especially likely for a child who is hyperactive or has difficulty paying attention.

# PAYING ATTENTION
# AND IMPROVING MEMORY

We all have a limited capacity to pay attention to information. Nobody can pay attention to everything that is happening around them. You want to review the learning situation and make sure the child focuses on its key elements. Watch how your child listens to information in the tutoring sessions. Often, children pay attention to irrelevant or meaningless information and don't focus on the important or salient elements. Highlight, emphasize, or review with your child what's important.

The type of information you present will also have a significant effect on how your child pays attention in the tutoring sessions. If the information presented to your child is too novel or unfamiliar, your child will likely have difficulty paying attention and remembering it. Always attempt to impart new information in a way that makes it easy for your child to pay attention. Typically, we tend to pay our best attention to information that is just a little bit different from what we already know.

Don't assume that just because your child has heard or seen something, it will be remembered later. For a child to remember a lesson, the information has to be directly relevant to prior knowledge on the topic or the child has to use creative memory strategies, called mnemonic devices. Don't assume that your child will be able to memorize information by simply repeating it over and over. Most children try to memorize information by repeating it in the way that it was presented. This type of rehearsal is usually ineffective for the child who is experiencing difficulty. This child needs to creatively rehearse the information. Creative repetition is much more effective than simply repeating the information over and over. Creative rehearsal typically involves the use of rhyming or visualizing what needs to be committed to memory. It leads to strong associations in your child's memory and makes it easier to memorize and recall the information for later use.

Most children under the age of eight do not realize that they have to use these memory strategies. For example, children under the age of eight often simply hope that they will remember what's required, but will not rehearse or use a memory strategy. They can be taught a creative rehearsal strategy but will only use it for the specific situation in which it is presented. They will not generalize the use of a memory strategy to other situations.

Your child's brain has amazing natural abilities that you can tap into by using several well-known techniques for enhancing memory. The following memory strategies are useful for working with a child who is experiencing difficulty paying attention to and remembering information presented in learning situations.

**1.** *Use visual imagery techniques whenever possible.*

Ask your child to make mental images of the materials to be learned. For example, when teaching math facts, ask the child to make a mental image of the math operation when attempting to solve it. In other words, with eyes closed the child should picture the numbers that need to be manipulated. Encourage your child to create visual images when exposed to information that needs to be remembered later on. Eventually, you want your child to create visual images to associate with learning facts.

**2.** *Use acronyms.*

An acronym is a group of letters that stands for a list of actions, words, or symbols. For example, when instructions or directions for a task are given, you could use an acronym like "SLLR" which stands for stop, look, listen, repeat. Your child should be encouraged to stop the current action, look at the person who is talking, listen to what is being said, and repeat the directions silently or aloud. Before a teaching sessions starts, the teacher or tutor could mention the word "sillier," which stands for "SLLR," and ask the child to repeat out loud what it stands for.

Acronyms are also useful for recalling specific types of information. For example, all fifty states could be remembered by making up a sentence that includes fifty letters with each one standing for a state. In written music, the sentence "Every good boy does fine" was developed to refer to the five lines in the treble clef that represent the notes E, G, B, D, and F.

**3.** *Use the method of loci.*

The method of loci is a mnemonic device used by the ancient Greeks. It involves:

• Making a mental sketch of a familiar place, such as one's house or room.

• Mentally traveling around the house.

• Associating an object in the house with an idea or word to be remembered. For example, a child who has to remember the first three presidents could imagine George Washington sleeping in the bed, John Adams eating breakfast at the kitchen table, and Thomas Jefferson sitting in the living room watching television.

**4.** *Use the "peg word" system:*
To use the "peg word" system, a child must first memorize the associations of the numbers one to ten in the following rhyme:

One is a sun, two is a shoe, three is a tree, four is a door, five is a hive, six are sticks, seven is heaven, eight is a gate, nine is a lime, and ten is a hen.

By using these rhyme associations it is possible to accurately remember a list of any number of items up to ten. To remember a list of groceries to buy at the store, such as butter, eggs, and mustard, the child could imagine:

- Butter melting outside from the sun (item 1).

- Broken eggs inside a shoe (item 2).

- Cans of mustard hanging on a Christmas tree (item 3).

**5.** *Train your child to take notes to keep track of assignments.*
Your child could also have an assignment book to help recall the work that must be completed.

**6.** *Encourage your child to consistently repeat back the directions for completing work.*
Repeating silently or out loud ensures that the child understands and does not forget the directions.

## COMPENSATORY STRATEGIES

Compensatory strategies are designed to soften the effect of the learning difficulty but cannot remove it. The assumption here is that the difficulties have a long-term existence, and that you will not be able to eliminate them in a short period of time. Examples of such difficulties are severe academic deficits where your child is several years below grade level, poor handwriting, problems paying attention, or being unable to work quickly. Instead of trying to eliminate these difficulties, you can develop strategies for working around them. You have to structure your child's learning environment so that it adjusts for the learning difficulties. For example:

1. *Make sure that your child's teachers are aware of attending limitations.*

   Sometimes teachers may view a child with difficulty paying attention as either academically deficient or willfully disobedient. It is important for you to coordinate with your child's teachers to arrest inaccurate misconceptions.

2. *Don't overload your child.*

   Break down the tasks into simple components. Eventually, you would like to train your child to be able to do this independently. You could practice breaking down tasks into their component parts with your child. The use of diagrams or pictures may be helpful.

3. *Try to have your child work in situations that offer a minimum of distraction.*

   If your child has difficulty paying attention, don't try to work together when the television is blasting nearby or other people are having a loud conversation.

4. *Teach your child to self-monitor performance.*

   The child could have a list of daily work activities and check off the ones that are successfully completed.

5. *Try to adjust the amount of written assignments.*

   Often children with fine motor or visual-motor difficulties cannot complete written assignments as quickly as their peers. Completing written assignments can be an extremely frustrating task for these children. It makes sense to decrease the amount of written assignments they have to complete. Reducing their workload may not significantly affect their amount of learning but will significantly decrease their frustration. Children don't necessarily have to complete twenty examples to learn a math skill. Five or ten well-constructed and reviewed examples could be sufficient for proper learning to occur.

6. *Provide your child with an opportunity to become computer literate.*

   The computer enables a child to compensate for poor handwriting or difficulties with writing.

**7.** *Remember that even some gifted children are poor spellers.*
If your child is a terrible speller, use inventive spelling strategies. Invented spelling is a process in which the child is told not to worry about the correct spelling of words but to focus on the content of the story being written. A child with poor spelling skills may avoid writing stories because of fear of spelling mistakes. If we eliminate that fear, it is more likely that the child will produce a greater quantity and quality of writing samples.

**8.** *Tutor your child in test-taking skills.*
Sometimes, children perform poorly on tests because they have weak test-taking skills, while others are excellent at guessing the types of questions that teachers will put on exams. You need to train your child to be a good predictor of the test questions. For example, you and your child could create hypothetical test questions and then later compare it to those in the real test.

# Things You Can Do

## EXERCISES

**1.** List situations in which your child could benefit significantly from your help and assistance.

**2.** List situations in which your child does not benefit from your help and assistance. Reevaluate your tutoring strategies and the types of materials you are using.

**3.** Meet with your child's teacher to coordinate your tutoring with the classroom lessons.

## QUESTIONS TO ASK YOURSELF

**1.** Do you feel that some topic areas are too difficult for you to tutor? If the answer is yes, you need to slow down and try to get more active assistance from your child and the teachers. Do only as much as you feel comfortable with.

**2.** Do you take breaks when either you or your child is tired?

**3.** Do you and your child have positive feelings about the tutoring sessions? If the answer is no, you and your child need to sit down and discuss ways of improving them.

# Appendix A

# RESOURCES AND ORGANIZATIONS

■ ■ ■

This section is devoted to providing parents with sources for information concerning their children's learning difficulties. A good place to start is with your state education department. An official at that department should explain the educational rights of your children and the obligation of the schools in your state. In addition, the official can suggest written sources for current information on children's learning difficulties. You could also contact a local college or university with an education department for the most current research in education.

If you decide to have a private individual tutor your child, be very careful about choosing one. It is best to stay away from private educational services that promise or guarantee spectacular results. The spectacular results often lead to spectacular costs without any significant educational benefits. Many unscrupulous individuals reap great financial rewards from parents desperate to improve their children's grades. Educational gains are usually the result of old-fashioned work and step-by-step progress. It is rare for a child with significant learning problems to obtain a quick and immediate cure.

I have worked with only one child who obtained an immediate cure for his reading problem. Joseph was referred to me by his third grade teacher because he had great difficulty reading. He wore bifocal glasses and often reversed words, read only parts of words, or skipped lines when reading. I asked Joseph to take off his glasses when reading for me, and he read significantly better. I then arranged for him to visit an ophthalmologist, who examined his eyes and glasses. It turned out that he had an incorrect prescription and did not know how to use his bifocals. He got a new prescription, learned to use the bifocals, and ended his reading difficulties. This was a very unusual situation. I have never had another one like it.

If you want a private reading tutor, you could contact your child's school or a local college. You may also want a school psychologist to work with the tutor to set up an individualized tutoring and educational program. The tutoring experience should be closely integrated with your child's classroom experience.

A list of national organizations that parents could contact for information on their child's learning difficulties follows. These are organizations that may be able to provide you with literature or referrals to professionals and support groups.

### ATTENDING DIFFICULTIES

Attention Deficit Disorders
Association (ADDA)
8091 South Ireland Way
Aurora, CO 80016

Children and Adults with
Attention Deficit
Disorders (CHADD)
499 N.W. 70th Avenue
Suite 109
Plantation, FL 33317

### GENERAL LEARNING DIFFICULTIES

Association for Children
With Learning Disabilities
(ACLD)
Library Road
Pittsburgh, PA 15234
(412) 341-8077

Association on
Handicapped Student
Service Programs in Post-
Secondary Education
(AHSSPPE)
P.O Box 21192
Columbus, OH 43221
(614) 488-4972

Center on Human Policy
Syracuse University
406 Huntington Hall
Syracuse, NY 13210
(315) 423-3851

Clearinghouse on the
Handicapped
Office of Special Education
and Rehabilitative
Services
U.S. Department of
Education
Switzer Building
Room 3132
Washington, DC 20202-
2319
(202) 732-1241

Closer Look?
Parents Campaign for
Handicapped Children and
Youth
1201 16th Street, N.W.
Washington, DC 20036
(202) 822-7900
(800) 522-3458 Learning
Disability teen line toll-
free number

Council for Exceptional
Children (CEC)
1920 Association Drive
Reston, VA 22091-1589
(703) 620-3660

Council for Learning
Disabilities (CLD)
9013 North Brooke Drive
Overland Park, KS 66212
(913) 492-3840

ERIC Clearinghouse on
Counseling and Personal
Services
University of Michigan
School of Education
Building
Room 2108
Ann Arbor, MI 48109
(313) 746-9492

ERIC Clearinghouse on
Elementary and Early
Childhood Education
University of Illinois
805 West Pennsylvania
Avenue
Urbana, IL 61801
(217) 333-1386

ERIC Clearinghouse on the
Handicapped and Gifted
Children
Council for Exceptional
Children
1920 Association Drive
Reston, VA 22091
(703) 620-3660

Foundation for Children
with Learning Disabilities
(FCLD)
P.O. Box 2929
Grand Central Station
New York, NY 10163
(212) 687-7211

International Reading
Association (IRA)
800 Barksdale Road
P.O. Box 940
Covington, LA 70434

Learning Disabilities
Association of America
4156 Library Road
Pittsburgh, PA 15234
(414) 341-1515

National Association of
Private Schools for
Exceptional Children
(NAPSEC)
2021 K Street, N.W.
Suite 315
Washington, DC 20006
(202) 296-1800

Orton Dyslexia Society
(ODS)
724 York Road
Baltimore, MD 21204
(410) 296-0232

Resources for Children
With Special Needs, Inc.
200 Park Avenue South
Suite 816
New York, NY 10003
(212) 677-4650

**VISION OR HEARING
IMPAIRMENT**

Books on Tape, Inc.
P.O. Box 7900
Newport Beach, CA 92660
(800) 626-3333

Junior National Association
of the Deaf (Jr. NAD)
445 North Pennsylvania
Suite 804
Indianapolis, IN 46204
(317) 638-1715 (voice and
TDD)

National Library Service for
the Blind and Physically
Handicapped
Library of Congress
1291 Taylor Street, N.W.
Washington, DC 20542
(202) 287-5100
(800) 424-8567

**GENERAL PHYSICAL
IMPAIRMENT**

Association of Birth Defect
Children (ABDC)
3526 Emerywood Lane
Orlando, FL 32806
(305) 859-2821

Asthma & Allergy
Foundation of America
(AAFA)
1835 K Street, N.W.
Suite P-900
Washington, DC 20006
(202) 293-2950

Epilepsy Foundation of
America (EFA)
4351 Garden City Drive
Suite 406
Landover, MD 20785
(301) 459-3700

Muscular Dystrophy
Association (MDA)
810 Seventh Avenue
New York, NY 10019
(212) 586-0808

National Down Syndrome
Congress (NDSC)
1640 West Roosevelt Road
Chicago, IL 60608
(312) 226-0416
(800) 446-3835

National Down Syndrome
Society
141 Fifth Avenue
New York, NY 10010
(212) 460-9330
(800) 221-4602

National Easter Seal Society
2023 West Ogden Avenue
Chicago, IL 60612
(312) 243-8400
(312) 243-8880 (TDD)
(800) 221-6827

National Genetics
Foundation, Inc. (NGF)
555 West 57th Street
New York, NY 10019
(212) 586-5900

National Head Injury
Foundation
333 Turnpike Road
Southboro, MA 01772
(617) 485-9950

United Cerebral Palsy
Associations (UCPA)
66 East 34th Street
New York, NY 10016
(212) 481-6300

**MISCELLANEOUS**

National Council on
Stuttering (NCOS)
P.O. Box 8171
Grand Rapids, MI 49508
(616) 241-2372

Tourette Syndrome
Association (TSA)
41-02 Bell Boulevard
Bayside, NY 11361
(718) 224-2999

**INTERVENTION PROGRAMS**

American Art Therapy
Association (AATA)
1980 Isaac Newton Square
South
Reston, VA 22090
(703) 437-6012

American Association for
Music Therapy
66 Morris Avenue
Springfield, NJ 07081
(201) 379-1100

American Association for
Rehabilitation Therapy
P.O. Box 93
North Little Rock, AR 72116

American Dance Therapy
Association (ADTA)
2000 Century Plaza
Suite 108
Columbia, MD 21044
(410) 997-4040

Project Head Start
Administration for
Children, Youth and Families
Office of Human
Development Services
U.S. Department of Health
and Human Services
P.O. Box 1182
Washington, DC 20013
(202) 755-7710

Sibling Information
Network
Connecticut's University
Affiliated Facility
University of Connecticut
249 Glenbrook Road U-64
Storrs, CT 06269
(203) 486-4034

# APPENDIX B

# SUGGESTED READING

■ ■ ■

The following are reading materials that may be helpful for parents seeking advanced knowledge concerning their child's learning difficulties.

### ATTENTION DEFICIT HYPERACTIVITY DISORDER

Barkley, R. A. 1990. *Attention Deficit Hyperactivity Disorder.* New York: Guilford Press.

Barkley, R. A. 1987. *Defiant Children: A Clinician's Manual to Parent Training.* New York: Guilford Press.

DuPaul, G. J., and Stoner, G. 1994. *ADHD in the Schools.* New York: Guilford Press.

Ingersoll, B. 1988. *Your Hyperactive Child.* New York: Doubleday.

Ingersoll, B., and Goldstein, S. 1994. *Attention Deficit Disorder and Learning Disabilities.* New York: Doubleday.

Moss, R. A. 1991. *Why Johnny Can't Concentrate.* New York: Bantam.

Parker, H. C. 1990. *The ADD-Hyperactivity Workbook.* Plantation, Florida: Impart Publications.

Silver, L. B. 1992. *The Misunderstood Child.* Blue Ridge Summit, Pa.: Tab Books.

Turecki, S., and Tonner, L. 1989. *The Difficult Child.* New York: Bantam.

Weiss, G., and Hechtman, L. T. 1993. *Hyperactive Children Grown Up.* New York: Guilford Press.

Wendler, P. 1987. *The Hyperactive Child, Adolescent, and Adult.* New York: Oxford University Press.

**LEARNING PROBLEMS**

Christenson, S., and Conoley, J. C. 1992. *Home-School Collaboration: Building a Fundamental Educational Resource.* Silver Spring, Md.: National Association of School Psychologists.

Coles, G. 1987. *The Learning Mystique.* New York: Fawcett Columbine.

Dodd, A. W. 1992. *A Parent's Guide to Innovative Education.* Chicago: Noble Press.

Graden, J. L., Zins, J. E., and Curtis, M. J. 1988. *Alternative Educational Delivery Systems: Enhancing Educational Options for All Students.* Silver Spring, Md.: National Association of School Psychologists.

Leeds, J. 1994. *Smart Questions to Ask About Your Children's Education.* New York: Harper Paperbacks.

Rosner, J. 1993. *Helping Children Overcome Learning Difficulties.* New York: Walter and Company.

Shephard, L. A., and Smith, M. L. 1989. *Flunking Grades: Research and Policies on Retention.* New York: Palmer Press.


**REVIEWS OF EDUCATIONAL MATERIALS**

Ellison, R. R. 1992. *Parents, Kids, and Computers.* New York: Random House.

Lipson, E. R. 1991. *New York Times Parent's Guide to the Best Books for Children,* 2nd ed. New York: Random House.

Oppenheim, J., Brenner, B., and Boegehold, B. D. 1986. *Choosing Books for Kids.* New York: Ballantine.

Zuckert, E. R. 1994. *The Kidstuff Survey.* New York: Cove Point Press.


**LEARNING STRATEGIES**

Greene, L. J. 1991. *1001 Ways to Improve Your Child's Schoolwork.* New York: Dell.

McCarney, S. B., and Bauer, A. M. 1991. *A Parent's Guide to Learning Disabilities.* Columbia, Mo.: Hawthorne.

Stoner, G., Shinn, M. R., and Hill, M. W. 1991. *Interventions for Achievement and Behavior Problems*. Silver Spring, Md.: National Association of School Psychologists.

Thomas, A., and Grimes, J. 1990. *Best Practices in School Psychology II*. Silver Spring, Md.: National Association of School Psychologists.

Weiner, A. S. 1990. *Any Child Can Read Better*. New York: Bantam.

## HOMEWORK PROBLEMS

Anesko, K. M., and Levine, F. M. 1987. *Winning the Homework War*. New York: Arco.

Clark, F., and Clark, C. 1989. *Hassle Free Homework*. New York: Doubleday.

## MOTIVATION-BEHAVIOR PROBLEMS

Bruns, J. H. 1992. *They Can But They Don't*. New York: Viking.

Dreikurs, R. 1964. *Children: The Challenge*. New York: Hawthorne/Dutton.

Faber, A., and Mazlish, E. H. 1980. *How to Talk So Kids Will Listen & Listen So Kids Will Talk*. New York: Avon Books.

Ginott, H. 1969. *Between Parent and Child*. New York: Avon Books.

Ginott, H. 1971. *Between Parent and Teenager*. New York: Avon Books.

Kurcinka, M. S. 1992. *Raising Your Spirited Child*. New York: Harper Perennial.

# Appendix C

# REFERENCES

■ ■ ■

Barkley, R. A. 1990. *Attention Deficit Hyperactivity Disorder: A Handbook for Diagnosis and Treatment.* New York: Guilford Press.

Davis, W. E. 1980. *Resource Guide to Special Education.* Boston: Allyn & Bacon.

Erikson, E. H. 1963. *Childhood and Society.* New York: Norton & Company.

*The FCLD Learning Disabilities Resource Guide.* 1985. New York: New York University Press.

Glass, G. V., Cohen, L. S., Smith, M. L., and Filby, N. N. 1982. *School Class Size: Research & Policy.* Beverly Hills, Calif.: Sage Publications.

Gordon, M. 1991. *ADD/Hyperactivity: A Consumer's Guide.* Dewitt, N.Y.: GSI Publications.

Happe, David. 1990. "Best Practices in Identifying Community Resources." In A. Thomas and J. Grimes (eds.), *Best Practices in School Psychology.* Washington, D.C.: National Organization of School Psychologists.

Harris, A. J., and Sipay, E. R. (1980). *How to Increase Reading Ability.* New York: Longman.

Holmes, C. T. 1989. "Grade Level Retention Effect: A Meta Analysis of Research Studies." In L. A. Shephard and M. L. Smith (eds.), *Flunking Grades: Research Policies on Retention.* New York: Palmer Press.

Parker, H. C. 1990. *The ADD-Hyperactivity Workbook*: Plantation, Florida: Impart Publications.

Pressley, M., Johnson, C. J., Symons, S., and McGoldrick, J. A. 1989. "Strategies That Improve Children's Memory and Comprehension of Text." *Elementary School Journal 90*, 3–32.

Rest, J. R. 1984. "The Major Components of Morality." In W. M. Kurtines and J. L. Gewirtz (eds.), *Morality, Moral Behavior, and Moral Development.* New York: John Wiley and Sons.

Seligman, M. E. P. 1975. *Helplessness: On Depression, Development and Death.* San Francisco: W. H. Freeman and Company.

Shephard, L. A., and Smith, M. L. 1989. *Flunking Grades: Research and Policies on Retention.* New York: Palmer Press.

Slavin, R. E. 1989a. "Grouping for Instruction in Elementary School." In R. E. Slavin (ed.), *School and Classroom Organization.* Hillsdale, N. J.: Lawrence Erlbaum.

Slavin, R. E. 1989b. "What Works for Students at Risk: A Research Synthesis." *Educational Leadership 46,* 4–14.

Slavin, R. E., Karweit, M. L., and Madden, N. A. 1989. *Effective Programs for Students At Risk.* Needham Heights, Mass: Allyn & Bacon.

U.S. Department of Education, Office of Special Education and Rehabilitative Services, National Institute of Handicapped Research. *Directory of National Information Services on Handicapping Conditions and Related Services.* 1986. Washington, D.C.: Author.